THE SELECTED POEMS OF

PO CHÜ-I

THE SELECTED POEMS OF

PO CHÜ-I

TRANSLATED BY
DAVID HINTON

A NEW DIRECTIONS BOOK

Acknowledgments: The translation of this book was supported by grants from the National Endowment for the Humanities and the Witter Bynner Foundation.

Manufactured in the United States of America
New Directions Books are published on acid-free paper.
First published as New Directions Paperbook 880 in 1999
Book design by Sylvia Frezzolini Severance
Map by Molly O'Halloran

Library of Congress Cataloging-in-Publication Data

Pai, Chü-i, 772–846
    [Poems. English. Selections]
    The selected poems of Po Chü-I / translated by David Hinton.
        p.   cm.
    "A New directions book."
    Includes bibliographical references.
    ISBN 0-8112-1412-5 (alk. paper)
    1. Pai, Chü-i, 772–846—Translations into English.
I. Hinton, David, 1954– .   II. title.
PL2674.A247   1999   99-12371
895.1'13–dc21   CIP

New Directions Books are published for James Laughlin
by New Directions Publishing Corporation,
80 Eighth Avenue, New York, NY 10011

CONTENTS

EXILE: 815-820

MIDDLE POEMS: 820-829

LATE POEMS: 829-846

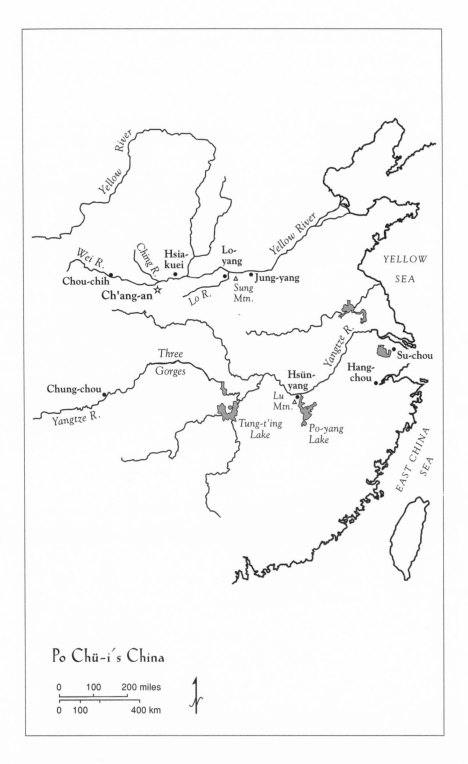

Po Chü-i's China

0   100   200 miles
0   100   400 km

INTRODUCTION

1.

In *The Analects*, Confucius says: "There are three hundred songs in *The Book of Songs*, but this one phrase tells it all: *thoughts never twisty*" (II.2). *The Book of Songs* is the ancient source from which the Chinese poetic tradition flows, and *thoughts never twisty* may very well describe the essence of the entire tradition as well, for it is a tradition that consistently valued clarity and depth of wisdom, not mere complexity and virtuosity. In this, Po Chü-i (772-846 C.E.) is the quintessential Chinese poet, for although it deeply informs the work of all the major ancient poets, Po makes that sage clarity itself his particular vision.

Po Chü-i was a more serious student of Ch'an (Zen) Buddhism than any mainstream poet up to his time, and it was Ch'an that gave much of the clarity and depth to his life and work. Po's poems often include the explicit use of Ch'an ideas, indeed he is the poet who really opened mainstream poetry to Buddhist experience, his work becoming a major source of information on Buddhist practice in his time. But it is in the poetics shaping Po's poetry that Ch'an is more fundamentally felt. In Ch'an practice, the self and its constructions of the world are dissolved away until nothing remains but empty mind or "no-mind." This empty mind is often spoken of as mirroring the world, leaving its ten thousand things utterly simple, utterly themselves, and utterly sufficient. That suggests one possible Ch'an poetry: an egoless poetry which renders the ten thousand things in such a way that they empty the self as they shimmer with the clarity of their own self-sufficient identity. Po wrote a number of poems in this mode, but the great master of this poetics was Wang Wei (699-759), whose brief poems resound with the selfless clarity of no-mind:

DEER PARK

No one to see. In empty mountains,
hints of drifting voice, no more.

Entering deep woods again, late
sunlight on green moss, rising.

    The other possibile Ch'an poetry is that of an egoless ego. Empty mind would seem to preclude the possibility of a personal poetry such as Po's. The quiet response of even the most reticent poem is still a construction, as Po knew well: he playfully says numerous times that his Ch'an practice has failed because he could not overcome his "poetry demon," his "word-karma." Po's response to experience seems to have been quite passionate– whether the experience was as monumental as poverty and war, or as ordinary as tea and an afternoon nap– and this full heart was of course the engine driving his prolific output as a poet. Po had hoped that Ch'an practice might quell his passionate responses, and this certainly did happen to some extent, but it seems he came to realize that the self is also one of those ten thousand things that are utterly themselves and suffi-cient. Taoist thought would describe this insight rather differently, as the real-ization that self is always already selfless, for it is but a momentary form among the constant transformation of earth's ten thousand things. This is a crucial con-junction of Ch'an and Taoist philosophy, and no doubt a major reason Po con-sidered them to be two aspects of the same system. In any case, this insight results in a poetry quite different from Wang Wei's. Rather than Wang Wei's strategy of losing the self among the ten thousand things, this poetics opens the poem to the various movements of self, and Po Chü-i was a master of its subtle ways. In a culture that made no fundamental distinction between heart and mind, he inhabited everyday experience at the level where a simple heart is a full heart and a simple mind is an empty mind, endowing *thoughts never twisty* with new depths. Such is his gentle power: the sense in his poems of dwelling at the very center of one's life, combining the intimacies of a full heart and the dis-tances of an empty mind. This is life invested with its richest dimensions, dimensions rendered visible in Chou Ch'en's "After Po Chü-i's Line: *Idle, Watching the Kids Catch Willow Blossoms*" (cover illustration).

    Po found his full heart and empty mind most completely realized in the practice of idleness. This idleness is also central to the work of T'ao Ch'ien (365-427), the poet who originated the poetic world which defines the Chinese tradition. Etymologically, the character for idleness which T'ao Ch'ien used (hsien) connotes "profound serenity and quietness," its pictographic elements rendering a tree standing alone within the gates to a courtyard, or in its alternate form, moonlight shining through an open door. Po Chü-i often uses this character as well, but he also uses another character: lan. The pictographic elements of this character are equally revealing: it is made up of the character for "trust" (lai) beside the character for "heart-mind" (hsin). Hence, the heart-mind of trust, the heart-mind of trust in the world. But this is trust of truly profound dimensions, for "idleness" is essentially a lazybones word for a spiritual posture known as wu-wei. Wu-wei is a central concept in Taoism, where it is associated with tzu-jan, the mechanism of Tao's process. Tzu-jan's literal meaning is "self-so" or "the of-itself" or "being such of itself," hence "spontaneous" or "natural." But a more descriptive translation might be "occurrence appearing of itself," for it is meant to describe the ten thousand things unfolding spontaneously, each according to its own nature. For Taoists, we dwell as an organic part of tzu-jan by practicing wu-wei, which literally means "nothing doing," or more descriptively, "selfless action": acting spontaneously as a selfless part of tzu-jan, rather than with self-conscious intention. Hence, idleness is a kind of meditative reveling in tzu-jan, a state in which daily life becomes the essence of spiritual practice.

Like T'ao Ch'ien's, Po Chü-i's idleness often takes the form of drinking. Drunkenness for Po means, as it generally does in Chinese poetry, drinking just enough wine to achieve a serene clarity of attention, a state in which the isolation of a mind imposing distinctions on the world gives way to a sense of identity with the world. And so again, idleness as a kind of spiritual practice: an utter simplicity of dwelling in which empty mind allows a full heart to move with open clarity. Indeed, Po Chü-i half-seriously spoke of wine rivaling Ch'an as a spiritual practice.

Given his devotion to idleness and the poetics of idleness, Po tends to avoid the kind of imagistic compression more typical of Chinese poetry. For him, the poem is generally a kind of relaxed rambling, open to all thought and experience, whether petty or profound. And not surprisingly, his poems are written in exceptionally clear and plain language. Indeed, there is a story that Po always showed his poems to an uneducated old servant-woman, and anything she couldn't understand he rewrote. This poetics also allowed Po to write easily: he wrote a very large number of poems (2800 survive, far more than any poet before him), and the vast majority of them appear plain and unaccomplished, no different from the work of countless other poets. His poetics suggest that for him such poems would be the most authentically accomplished, for it no doubt reverses the normal criterion for poetry, making poems that are simple and unaccomplished valued above those that push to extremes in shaping experience. But Po doesn't resist the insight that makes striking poems. Surpising insight comes to some of his poems and not to others, and it makes sense that Po doesn't choose among them. So there is a body of poems which walk the fine line where a poem is effortlessly plain and yet surprising and insightful, revealing the profound dimensions of Po's trust in the simple and immediate. Even though there is a risk of misrepresenting Po Chü-i, it is primarily these poems that are presented in this book.

Po Chü-i wrote during the T'ang Dynasty, the period during which Chinese poetry experienced its first great flowering. This renaissance began during the High T'ang period (712-760) in the work of such poets as Wang Wei, Li Po, and Tu Fu, and continued through the Mid-T'ang period (766-835) during which Po Chü-i wrote. Though it hardly ignores life's hardships, the Chinese tradition is grounded in a poetry of balanced affirmation, its great poets speaking primarily of their immediate experience in a natural voice. But while Po Chü-i was cultivating his pellucid sensibility into the quintessence of this mainstream tradition, a group of poets was experimenting with an alternative poetics which became the most distinctive development during the Mid-T'ang– a poetics of startling disorientations and dream-like hermeticism. This alternative tradition began in the dark extremities of Tu Fu's later work. This work extended the mainstream tradition to its limit, and the stark introspective depths of Meng Chiao's late work (807-814) mark a clear break. Indeed, Meng Chiao's quasi-surreal and symbolist techniques anticipated landmark developments in the modern western tradition by a millennium, and it is interesting to reconsider the modern avant-garde in light of the alternative Mid-T'ang movement. After Meng Chiao, this movement included a number of major poets and at least two great ones: Li Ho and Li Shang-yin. But its vitality proved rather short-lived, ending with Li Shang-yin's death in 858, though its preoccupations remained dominant for another century, through the feeble Late-T'ang period (836-907), and the reverence accorded its major poets didn't begin to wane for another two centuries. The alternative tradition of Meng Chiao and his heirs made the Mid-T'ang (766-835) an especially rich poetic period, rivaling even its predesessor, the illustrious High T'ang. But Po Chü-i's unassuming poetics proved more enduring than the experimental alternative, for although such poetics result in a modest poetry, it reflects a deep wisdom that was always more admired in China than mere virtuosity and innovation. It was largely through the work of Po Chü-i and other more "conventional" Mid-T'ang poets that the tradition's mainstream was passed on to the next great period of Chinese poetry: the Sung Dynasty, a period in which Ch'an's widespread influence led to a poetry that continued to deepen and expand the possibilities of *thoughts never twisty*.

2.

Born into the lower levels of the educated bureaucratic class and for some reason raised primarily by relatives rather than his parents, Po Chü-i lived in unsettled poverty as a youth. After a childhood spent in several northern towns, he was taken southeast at twelve or thirteen, a refugee from drought, famine, and the civil unrest that was ravaging China at the time. The grand T'ang Dynasty was foundering badly as a result of the An Lu-shan rebellion (755-63) and the chronic militarism it spawned. Of the country's 53 million people, the rebellion left 36 million either dead or living as displaced refugees. The central government was crippled by factionalism and palace intrigue, and fighting off external threats continued to weaken it, while vast outlying regions were lost. At the same time, much of China itself splintered into dozens of semi-autonomous regions ruled by warlords having no loyalty to the emperor, and the fighting between these warlords and the central government devastated the populace through unmanageable taxation, heavy conscription, and the widespread destruction of battle. The empire's chaotic fragmentation continued throughout Po Chü-i's life, and twenty years after his death in 846, a massive peasant rebellion began which finally led to the T'ang's collapse in 907.

The chaotic social situation kept Po's life unsettled and difficult enough– but then, when he was twenty-four, his father died. At that point, the family's poverty became severe: it is reported that they had no place to live and were forced to beg for food and clothes. It seems Po often worked at petty bureaucratic jobs to help support the family. But he had received a classical education, showing great promise from his earliest years, and he somehow managed to keep up his studies and work as a poet. In his late twenties, Po passed the extremely difficult national examinations which qualified men for high government position, thus securing for himself the promise of an illustrious political career. Because of his difficult circumstances, Po took these exams much later than usual, but given that only a handful of men passed each year, his success is a testament to his talent and diligence. The group of candidates who passed in Po's year became close friends and allies, rising to the highest levels of government and forming a major political force in Chinese politics over the next half century.

Po Chü-i formed a legendary friendship with one colleague in particuliar: Yüan Chen, who also rose from difficult circumstances and shared Po Chü-i's political and poetic outlook. Their friendship was strong and enduring, though they spent rather little time together: there were several years when they both lived in Ch'ang-an, the capital, but otherwise they met only four times, spending a few days together each time. They both became very popular as poets, and to sustain their friendship through long periods of separation, they relied on poetry. Their poems were among the first secular texts to be mechanically printed and distributed in large numbers. They were read by emperors, officials, and monks, sung by courtesans in wine houses, and copied out by school children. Po's popularity even extended to Japan. Not surprisingly, this popularity was not based on the poems which proved to have the most lasting value. Instead, it was due to his simple style and his poems of sentiment: those he exchanged with Yüan Chen, for instance, and two long and oft-cited ballads, "The Song of Unending Sorrow" and "The Song of the P'i-P'a," which hold relatively little interest for us at this distance.

After a brief appointment in Chou-chih, west of Ch'ang-an, Po rose through several positions in the capital and became an advisor to the emperor at the age of thirty-six (808), a position he held for two years. Po was more active and forceful in influencing national policy during these years than at any other time in his life, and he clearly had not forgotten the experience of his youth, for he was adamant and outspoken in his defense of the long-suffering common people, attacking injustice and government malfeasance. Finding their official efforts hampered by conservative elements that controlled the central administration, Po and Yüan Chen decided to use their widely-circulated poetry to further their cause. Declaring poetry's highest purpose to be the instigation of social change, they attempted to revive the ancient tradition of the *yüeh-fu*. Folk songs often critical of the government, *yüeh-fu* are said to have been collected by noble ancient rulers in order to gauge the sentiments of the common people and so improve their ability to govern. This supposedly happened all the way back to the mythical times of the sage-emperor Yao (regnant 2357-2255 B.C.E.). *The Book of Songs* was said to be Confucius' collection of such poems (fifth century B.C.E.), and the term *"yüeh-fu"* (meaning "Music Bureau") derives from the first century B.C.E. when they were collected by the Han emperor Wu's Music Bureau. *Yüeh-fu* grew from a folk into a literary form, and many poets over the centuries wrote *yüeh-fu* on occasion, but Po's series of fifty "New *Yüeh-fu*" (pp. 18-27) and ten "Songs of Ch'in-chou" (pp. 30-31) together represent the most programmatic and historically influential instance. They were a systematic attempt to return poetry to the moral dimensions of *The Book of Songs*, and they had a very real political force as well. As Po's poetry was read and sung throughout the land, his "New *Yüeh-fu*" not only directly and forcefully influenced the emperor, they also stirred up popular indignation and broad support for reforms. This made them a double affront against conservative elements in the administration.

In 811 Po's mother died, and according to custom, Po resigned his government position and entered a three-year period of mourning. Po left the capital and lived as something of a recluse for the next three years in Hsia-kuei, where his family had a farm because it was their ancestral village. This was the first extended period of time Po had had for quiet reflection, and that reflection was intensified not only by his mother's death, but also by his chronic illness and the sudden death of his only child, a three-year-old daughter. Although these were not happy years, it seems that in this period Po began to admit he was more of a recluse by nature than a dynamic statesman. This realization was no doubt facilitated by his political situation. The repercussions from his activism had apparently begun already, for he seems to have left the government with no hope of returning to his political career. Po must have realized that his stance was dangerous, and decided it wasn't worth the personal risk, for these years in Hsia-kuei reveal the beginning of a decisive shift away from political activism. He would always doubt the wisdom and authenticity of this shift, but never essentially change it. Po served in government for his entire life, but he avoided controversy and preferred appointments away from contentious capital politics. As a poet, he wrote very few political poems after this period, and those he did write weren't likely to offend his powerful opponents in government.

But political pressures aside, there is little doubt that Po was by nature a recluse and not a bureaucrat. He found routine government work intolerable and generally sought the least demanding positions, positions that left him plenty of time and energy for the solitude and reflection that the recluse poet in him needed. Po's poetry also makes it clear where his real commitments lay: he wrote a great many poems in his social roles, but it is almost always the poems of solitary reflection that probe deepest. It was also in Hsia-kuei that he began to establish the philosophical depths of his poetics of idleness. Like all intellectuals of his time, he was well-versed in the thought and practice of Taoism and Ch'an, but it was in Hsia-kuei that he began to seriously explore these spiritual dimensions. And upon his return to Ch'ang-an, he began to study with Ch'an masters. The Taoist/Ch'an philosophy of acceptance certainly answered to Po's recluse nature, and together they assured his political detachment.

Because Po had offended powerful factions in the capital, he returned after mourning to a fairly insignificant position, and little more than a year later he was exiled to Hsün-yang in the south. A mild form of exile, typical for those out of favor in the capital, this was essentially a transfer away from the policy-making center, for Po was given a position as Chief Magistrate in Hsün-yang with no loss of rank. But psychologically, this was indeed an exile, and Po seems to have taken the warning to heart, for his years in Hsün-yang complete his shift from political activism to private spiritual cultivation.

The Hsün-yang region had an especially rich cultural and spiritual heritage, and with a very undemanding position Po took advantage of it. Nearby Lu Mountain (literally "Thatch-Hut Mountain" or "Hermitage Mountain") had been a major monastic center for half a millennium, attracting many reclusive intellectuals, and it was the locus of a substantial literature. It was in Lu Mountain monasteries that the first glimmers of Ch'an became visible in China during the fourth and fifth centuries C.E., a time when two of China's greatest poets frequented the mountains and their monasteries: T'ao Ch'ien and Hsieh Ling-yün. Po was often to be found at these monasteries as he deepened his practice, thus establishing an intimate involvement with the monastic community that would last to the end of his life. He often wandered the mountains, and eventually fell in love with one particular site in a high valley below Incense-Burner Peak. There he built his famous "thatch hut," (pp. 62-65), a spiritual refuge where he spent a good deal of his time. Although he had renounced the moral intent of *The Book of Songs*, he now cultivated its more fundamental politics of simplicity in his poetry, investing *thoughts never twisty* with profound new dimensions.

After leaving Hsün-yang in 818, Po's political fortunes steadily ascended. He was first transferred and promoted to a kind of lesser banishment in Chung-chou, where he was Prefect of Chung Prefecture. Then, after less than two years there, he returned to Ch'ang-an when a new emperor who admired his poetry ascended the throne. This must have been an especially promising moment because the emperor also admired Yüan Chen's writing and Yüan had already been recalled from exile, meaning Po and Yüan would be together again in the capital. It was also promising because the poetry that the emperor especially admired was their political poetry. But this promise proved illusory. Although Yüan was appointed Chief Minister for a time, he was exiled within a year; and in 822, wanting to get clear of the fierce and dangerous factionalism in capital politics, Po arranged a transfer to Hang-chou in the southwest. There he served as Prefect, a choice assignment in a lovely location free of the fighting that engulfed much of China, and also one which did not require a great deal of work, thus allowing him ample time to cultivate his way of idleness. He returned north in 824, to a sinecure he arranged in Lo-yang. There he bought a very comfortable house with several acres of gardens. Po called this home for the rest of his life, but it would be several more years before he finally settled there.

In the meantime, he was appointed Prefect in Su-chou, another choice position, but one which proved very taxing. His always troubling health deteriorated, especially his eyes. He left after a year and a half, with the intention of retiring to his home in Lo-yang. But another promising new emperor suddenly came to power, so Po returned to the capital. Finally, after two years in the capital, Po realized this new emperor was more of the same and so returned to his Lo-yang sinecure in 829. He settled there for the seventeen remaining years of his life, living mostly as a kind of urban recluse. With the exception of three years as mayor of Lo-yang, he had few official demands on his time in Lo-yang. This was an ideal situation for Po: he was living in perfect recluse surroundings with few distractions or demands on his time, well-paid to single-mindedly cultivate his pellucid recluse ways.

But these years of tranquility were not undisturbed. In 831, Yüan Chen passed away. And that same year, Po's one-year-old son also died. This meant that, leaving aside several nephews and neices whom Po raised, only one of perhaps four children had survived infancy. Po's poor health continued to deteriorate, and in 839 he had a stroke which left him partially crippled. Then, in 842, the government began a campaign to suppress the Buddhist monastic system, causing considerable suffering among the monastic community that was so large a part of Po's life. Until 845, the campaign seemed a somewhat reasoned attempt to eliminate the widespread abuses of this system and recover some of the vast wealth that was ensconced in the tax-exempt monastic realm. That year, knowing his death was near, Po Chü-i assembled a final collection of his complete writings and placed copies in several prominent monasteries, thinking that was the safest way to preserve them. But only a few months later, the anti-Buddhist campaign escalated dramatically into the most widespread and destructive repression in pre-modern history. In less than a year, virtually all the monasteries in China were destroyed, and in the ashes lay the collections Po had so carefully worked to preserve. Other collections of Po's poetry existed in private hands, but as a result of the suppression, nearly all the work of Po's last three and a half years was lost. Only a handful of poems punctuate the silence that fills what would have been the last twenty pages of this book. But this may in the end be the clearest expression of his particular genius, for his voice seems hardly different from his silence.

EARLY POEMS: 794-815

HSIANG-YANG TRAVELS, THINKING OF MENG
HAO-JAN

Emerald Ch'u mountain peaks and cliffs,
emerald Han River flowing full and fast:

Meng's writing survives here, its elegant
ch'i now facets of changing landscape.

But today, chanting the poems he left us
and thinking of him, I find his village

clear wind, all memory of him vanished.
Dusk light fading, Hsiang-yang empty,

I look south to Deer-Gate Mountain, haze
lavish, as if some fragrance remained,

but his old mountain home is lost there:
mist thick and forests all silvered azure.

PEONY BLOSSOMS: SENT TÓ THE SAGE MONK CHENG I

Today, in front of the steps, these peonies out in such full red bloom:
how many of their blossoms are old now, and how many still young?

As they open, I can't think of comparisons to describe their color,
and as they fall, I'm just beginning to see we're the shapes of mirage

when they scatter through the Empty Gate into how many distances.
I wanted to gather a few withered petals, ask some sage about them.

LATE AUTUMN, DWELLING IN IDLENESS

My gate overgrown in this isolate land, greetings and farewells rare,
I loosen my robe and sit in idleness, nurturing the mystery of solitude.

This autumn courtyard's never swept. Finding myself a walking-stick,
I just amble and stroll all idleness here among yellow *wu-t'ung* leaves.

AFTER THE REBELLION, AT LIU-KOU MONASTERY

In this ninth month, all that Hsü-chou fighting ended yet again,
an agony of wild *ch'i*-ravaging wind fills rivers and mountains.

There's nothing left– just this monastery below Liu-kou Mountain,
and before the gates, same as ever, teeming scraps of white cloud.

AUTUMN THOUGHTS, SENT FAR AWAY

We share all these disappointments of failing
autumn a thousand miles apart. This is where

autumn wind easily plunders courtyard trees,
but the sorrows of distance never scatter away.

Swallow shadows shake out homeward wings.
Orchid scents thin, drifting from old thickets.

These lovely seasons and fragrant years falling
lonely away– we share such emptiness here.

HARD TIMES

Watch morning suns rise into heaven
and evening suns sinking into earth

and you don't notice it in the bright
mirror: but here I am, suddenly 34.

Don't say this body of mine isn't old.
It's getting there slowly, bit by bit,

and if white hair hasn't grown in yet,
that young face has begun giving way.

However long this life may endure,
I'll never be more than a visitor here:

though we're promised seventy years,
not one or two in ten lives them out,

so why always on my way somewhere
and always finding myself nowhere

near awakened? This inch-wide heart
is a treasure-hoard of boundless *ch'i*.

It's true poverty is a wretched thing,
but mastering Tao you abide in Tao,

and it's true wealth is a joyous thing,
but if it comes, it comes when it will.

Whatever brings deep wisdom to mind,
it's here in these things, nowhere else:

just sip a nice wine, and by day's end,
a little drunk, you're perfectly happy.

These words wear better than gold or jade.
Try them on and you'll never lose them.

WRITTEN IN SPRING ON A WALL AT FLOWERING-BRIGHTNESS MONASTERY

A princess who played her flute here followed the sage phoenix away,
leaving this refuge of immortals for what? It's *Flowering-Brightness*,

but is there anywhere all this falling-blossom sorrow can be endured?
In the meditation hall: an old white-haired monk sweeping the shadows.

AT WESTERN-CLARITY MONASTERY IN THE SEASON OF BLOOMING PEONIES, THINKING OF YÜAN CHEN

Last year we wrote our names on a wall
here, and now I come gazing at flowers.

A single job in rue-scented archives,
and I've seen peonies open three times,

but how can I cherish these blossoms
alone, this old-age blindness setting in,

or go looking for you, my garden friend
gone to Lo-yang and still not returned?

And such late spring thoughts opening
all distance here beside fragrant reds . . .

AT FLOWERING-BRIGHTNESS MONASTERY IN YUNG-CH'UNG DISTRICT

It's late summer weather, time bitter
heat begins to ease: windblown trees

murmur under skies promising rain,
and at dusk, cicadas cry on and on.

Narrow Yung-ch'ung streets quiet,
temple gardens all isolate mystery,

no one visits. Autumn scholartree
blossoms blanket the ground. Here,

the lit years pass, careless and slow,
the world's great dramas far away.

Why wait until I'm feeble to realize
our life's elusive, our death repose?

A true recluse need not live far away
knowing Tao is groping in darkness:

even in the world's bustle and dust
a mind of emptiness never wanders.

Fresh vegetables for dawn hunger
and fur-lined robes for chill nights:

such luck to elude hunger and cold.
What more could I ever ask? Simple

and hardly sick– this is all I want.
Rejoice in heaven, resent nothing:

how could I explain such resolve?
An *I Ching*'s lying beside the bed.

WANDERING AT CLOUD-DWELLING MONASTERY

Deep beneath a confusion of peaks, wandering among wildflowers
together on Cloud-Dwelling Road, we alone cherish all this spring.

It's a land of such beauty, and there's never been lord or master here.
Mountain realms are themselves a mountain monk's tender welcome.

COLD NIGHT IN THE COURTYARD

Dew-stained bamboo seems like jade,
and blown curtain-shadow like waves.

As I grieve over falling leaves, bright
moons in the courtyard grow countless.

THE SOUND OF PINES

The moon's beautiful, and sitting alone
beautiful. In two pines near the porch,

a breeze arrives from the southwest,
stealing into the branches and leaves,

swelling such isolate silence into sound
past midnight under a brilliant moon:

a cold mountain rain whispering far,
a cystalline *ch'in* pitched autumn pure.

I hear it rinsing summer heat clean,
clearing the confusion twilight darkens,

and by the end of a night without sleep,
body and mind are so light and quick.

Horses and carts soon crowd the road,
neighbors start their raucous flutesong.

Who'd believe it– here under the eaves,
ears so full and no trace of such racket?

FAREWELL TO THE RECLUSE WANG

An emperor's home always boasts wine,
and a noble's home always boasts meat.

For hosts of such high pride and renown,
the ritual minimum won't do for guests:

if someone arrives dust-covered, bowing,
the house bustles around day and night.

But you're shaking your robes out alone.
A cloud-crane setting out, you'd rather

go back home, white clouds and beyond,
sip streamwater, sleep in empty valleys.

Never following along with the crowd,
hands folded quietly, gaze turned down,

you knock at my gate to offer farewells.
I pour wine and invite you for the night,

a man leaving happily to feast on ferns,
those Chung-nan Mountains true green.

NEW YÜEH-FU

9. THE OLD MAN FROM HSIN-FENG WITH A BROKEN ARM

A frail and ancient man from Hsin-feng, eighty-eight years old,
hair and eyebrows white as fresh snow: he slowly makes his way

toward the inn's front gate, leaning on a great-great-grandson,
his left arm over the boy's shoulder, his right broken at his side.

If you ask this old man how many years his arm's been broken,
if you ask how it happened, an arm broken like that, he'll say:

When I was born at my home village in the district of Hsin-feng,
it was an age of sage rule, never a hint of wartime campaigns,

so I grew up listening to the flutes and songs of the Pear Garden,
knowing nothing at all about spears and flags, bows and arrows.

Then suddenly, in the T'ien-pao reign, they began building armies,
and for every three men in every household, one was taken away,

taken and hurried away. And can you guess where they all went?
To Yün-nan, a march five months and ten thousand miles long,

a march everyone kept talking about: how you face the Lu River
and malarial mists that rise and drift when pepper blossoms fall,

how great armies struggle to cross the river's seething floodwaters,
and before they makes it across, two or three in ten are drowned.

North of home, south of home, wailing filled villages everywhere,
sons torn from fathers and mothers, husbands torn from wives,

for people knew what it meant to make war on southern tribes:
ten million soldiers are sent away, and not one comes back alive.

It was all so long ago. I was hardly even twenty-four back then,
but my name was listed on those rolls at the Department of War,

so in the depths of night, careful to keep my plan well-hidden,
I stole away, found a big rock, and hacked my arm until it broke.

Too lame to draw a bow or lift banners and flags into the wind,
I escaped: they didn't send me off to fight their war in Yün-nan.

It was far from painless, the bone shattered and muscles torn,
but I'd found a way to go back and settle quietly in my village.

Now sixty years have come and gone since I broke this arm:
I gave up a limb, it's true, but I'm still alive, still in one piece,

though even now, on cold dark nights full of wind and rain,
I'm sleepless all night long with pain and still awake at dawn.

Sleepless with pain
but free of regrets,
for I'm the only man in my district who lived to enjoy old age.

If I hadn't done it, I'd have ended where the Lu River begins,
a dead body, my spirit adrift and my bones abandoned there,

just one of ten thousand ghosts drifting above southern graves,
gazing toward their home, all grief-torn and bleating, bleating.

When such elders speak
how can we ignore them?

Haven't you heard
the story of Sung K'ai-fu, Prime Minister in the K'ai-yüan reign,
how he nurtured peace by refusing to reward frontier victories?

Haven't you heard
the story of Yang Kuo-chung, Prime Minister in the T'ien-pao,
how he launched frontier campaigns to flatter the emperor,

how the people were wild with anger before he won anything?
Just ask him, ask the old man from Hsin-feng with a broken arm.

22. HUNDRED-FIRE MIRROR

Hundred-fire mirror
poured molten into molds like no other
as the morning sun rose in a land of gods and spirits,

cast and cooled on a boat in the heart of Yangtze rapids
on the fifth day of the fifth month under a midday sun:

it was polished pure with red-jade powder in golden oils
until it shimmered jewel-bright, a pool of autumn water.

Finally ready, it was presented at the Immortality Palace,
the finest in a long history of Yang-chou masterpieces,

but in our peopled world, its back ninety-five dragons
filling heaven with flight, it won't reflect human faces.

In awe, people say only a Son of Heaven can see into it.
I've even heard it once belonged to Emperor T'ai-tsung,

but T'ai-tsung always looked to the people for his mirror.
People reflecting past and present, never appearances:

that mirror's at hand everywhere in danger or peace,
hangs poised in mind as a hundred emperors rule chaos,

sure sign a Son of Heaven's mirror is nothing like this
perfect Yang-chou bronze tempered in a hundred fires.

24. TWIN VERMILLION GATES

Twin vermillion gates
facing each other north and south:

if you ask whose homes they could be,
people tell you all about two princes

playing flutes amid the five clouds of entanglement
as they rise into heaven transformed with immortality.

Their royal terraces and pavilions stayed behind here
in this human realm, reborn as Buddhist monasteries:

lady chambers and courtesan towers empty and silent,
willows like dancing waists beside ponds like mirrors.

Blossoms scatter in stillness. Dusk yellows in stillness.
You never hear songs anymore, only bells and chimes,

words to inspire carved in eloquent gold at the gates,
courtyards for monks and nuns all spacious elegance.

Full of idleness aplenty, green moss and bright moons,
they haunt a neighborhood of ragged homeless people,

and remember the one they've begun in P'ing-yang,
swallowing how many homes so simple and penniless?

With all these immortals leaving monasteries behind,
this human realm will soon vanish into Buddha palaces.

29. CRIMSON-WEAVE CARPET

Crimson-weave carpet,

silk reeled off select cocoons and boiled in clear water,
sun-bleached and steeped in dyes of crimdigo flower,

dyes turning thread crimson, indigo depths of crimson,
then woven to grace the Hall of Widespread Fragrance.

The Hall of Widespread Fragrance is a hundred feet long,
and the carpet's crimson weave will stretch end to end,

its iridescence soft and deep, its fragrance everywhere,
plush weave and mirage blossoms beyond all compare,

awaiting beautiful women who come to sing and dance,
gauze stockings and embroidered slippers sinking deep.

Even those carpets from T'ai-yüan seem stiff and rough,
and Ch'eng-tu rugs thin, their embroidered flowers cold:

they'll never compare to these, so warm and sumptuous
and sent each year from Hsüan-chou in the tenth month.

Hsüan-chou's grand Prefect orders a new pattern woven,
saying they'll spare no effort on the emperor's behalf,

and then a hundred reverent men haul it into the palace,
the weave so thick and silk so lavish it can't be rolled up.

Can you fathom what it means, O prefect of Hsüan-chou:
for ten feet of carpet
a thousand taels of silk?

Floors don't feel the cold– people do. People need warmth.
No more floors dressed in clothes stolen from the people.

30. AN OLD MAN OF TU-LING

An old man of Tu-ling scraping by in Tu-ling
planted his crops yet again this year, a hundred desolate acres,

but the rains didn't come in the third month, just a dry wind,
so his promising wheat fields just withered yellow and died,

then autumn cold came early, frost falling in the ninth month,
before millet had ripened, leaving seed-clusters burned black.

The magistrate saw it all, but instead of sending in for relief,
he gathered taxes ruthlessly, hoping to impress the capital,

so I pawned my mulberry groves and sold my land for taxes.
Now what? Where will food come from next year, or clothes?

They strip clothes from our backs
and steal food from our mouths,

terrorizing people and ravaging things like a pack of wolves.
Such savage talons and sawtooth jaws— what makes them feed on human flesh?

Finally someone reported the brutal scheme to our emperor,
and knowing people's duplicity, his heart full of compassion,

the emperor issued his sage resolution on white linen paper,
and the capital district was suddenly free of taxes for the year.

Yesterday, a clerk sent from the village arrived at our gates
carrying the royal proclamation to be posted in the hamlets,

but of every ten families, nine had already paid out their tax,
so it was emptiness that welcomed our noble lord's love here.

32. AN OLD CHARCOAL SELLER

An old charcoal seller
cuts firewood and sears it to charcoal below South Mountain,

his face smeared with dust and ash the color of woodsmoke,
his hair gone grizzled and grey, his ten fingers utter black,

and yet daring such hopes for the profits he'll take home
once the charcoal's all sold: warm robes to wear, food to eat.

His clothes are worn so miserably thin, and yet he worries
charcoal's selling too cheap, so he hopes for colder weather,

then one night an inch of snow falls in the city's foothills
and at dawn he takes his cart crackling through ruts of ice.

A tired ox and hungry man: the sun is already high when
they pause to rest in marketplace mud outside the south gate

and two riders no one knows appear in a dashing flourish:
one an envoy dressed in yellow, the other a servant in white.

The envoy carries an imperial warrant, and after reading it out,
he chases the ox away, turns the cart and takes it off north.

A cart like that easily carries a thousand pounds of charcoal,
but a palace envoy hurries it away without a second thought:

half a length of crimson lace and a few yards of fine damask
draped over the old ox's neck: isn't that a fair enough price?

46. A DRAGON IN THE DARK LAKE

The dark lake is bottomless, and its water shaded deep as black ink.
Legend says a dragon god dwells there, though no one's ever seen it,

so the magistrate built a shrine for daily sacrifices beside the lake:
A dragon will never be a god unless people themselves make it a god.

Prosperity and ruin, floodwater and drought, sickness and plague:
now the village believes this dragon controls everything that happens,

so penniless families fatten suckling pigs and strain clear wine for it.
Mornings they pray. Evenings their shaman calls to it with offerings:

and the dragon comes, O the wind sweeping in so tender and graceful,
rustling paper money, O so gently buffeting the brocade umbrellas,

and when the dragon leaves, O the wind grows still and quiet again,
incense flames failing, O plates and winecups slowly turning cold.

Shoreline rocks piled with meat,
shrine grasses soaked with wine:

no one knows how much of this the dragon god welcomes and savors,
but forest squirrels and mountain foxes always seem plump and tipsy.

Why please foxes?
Why punish pigs?
Year after year they slaughter suckling pigs and feed them to foxes,

and while happy foxes help themselves to its savory pigs, does it know
what's going on– a dragon at home in deep springs and nine distances?

ON MY DAUGHTER'S FIRST BIRTHDAY

Finally, after almost forty years of life,
I have a girl. We named her Golden-Bells,

and it's been a year since she was born.
Saying nothing, she studies sitting now,

but it seems I'm no sage-master at heart.
I can't get free of this trifling affection:

I know it's only a tangle of appearance,
but however empty, it's bliss to see her.

I'll worry about her dying. Spared that,
I'll worry about finding a good husband.

All those plans to find a mountain home:
I guess they'll wait another fifteen years.

NIGHT IN THE PALACE WITH CH'IEN HUI

When the water-clock sounds three times, I realize it's midnight.
Lovely wind and cold moonlight everywhere in pine and bamboo,

we sit here in perfect idleness, empty and still, saying nothing:
just two people in the shadows of a medicine tree, just two people.

SONGS OF CH'IN-CHOU

7. LIGHT AND SLEEK

Riding proud in the streets, parading
horses that glisten, lighting the dust . . .

When I ask who such figures could be,
people say they're imperial favorites:

vermillion sashes– they're ministers;
and purple ribbons– maybe generals.

On horses passing like drifting clouds
they swagger their way to an army feast,

to those nine wines filling cup and jar
and eight dainties of water and land.

After sweet Tung-t'ing Lake oranges
and mince-fish from a lake of heaven,

they've eaten to their hearts' content,
and happily drunk, their spirits swell.

There's drought south of the Yangtze:
in Ch'ü-chou, people are eating people.

10. BUYING FLOWERS

Late spring in this emperor's city,
horses and carts clattering past:

it's peony season on the avenues
and the people stream out to buy.

They won't be this cheap for long.
At these prices, anyone can buy.

Showing five delicate whites amid
hundreds of huge luminous reds,

they rig canopies to shelter them
and bamboo screens to shield them,

sprinkle them, stand them in mud,
keeping their color rich and fresh.

Families come back day after day:
people just can't shake their spell.

Happening by the flower markets,
an old man from a farm somewhere

gazes down and sighs to himself,
a sigh no one here could fathom:

a single clutch of bottomless color
sells for taxes on ten village farms.

EARLY MORNING, COMBING MY HAIR OUT

I wash it at night and comb it out early
(window lit, mirror all autumn dawn):

a single handful of hair long and thin,
and every bath leaving it thinner still.

The gradual bustle of years slips away,
tangling me in this world's tender ties.

Never mastering empty-gate dharma,
who can manage the ravages of age,

and without unborn mind, white hair
means a life unlived, a death too young.

MOURNING PEACH BLOSSOMS IN THE PALACE GARDENS
AT NIGHT, I THINK OF CH'IEN HUI

When I went home yesterday, these blossoms had just opened red.
I'm back again tonight, but already the branches are half empty.

And while I sit mourning ravaged blossoms you never saw bloom,
a sudden wind scatters the rest through blazing moonlight away.

IN SICKNESS, MOURNING GOLDEN-BELLS

What can I do? So sick, and your life
cut so short pitching me into such grief:

it startles me from sleep. I get up and try
lamplight for comfort against these tears,

but a daughter's an absolute tangle of love,
and without a son the sorrow's inescapable.

After three full years of nurture and care,
a sickness barely lasting ten quick days:

such things tear at the heart long after
tears follow the last cries of grief away.

Little robes still hung on dressing-racks,
the useless medicines there at your pillow,

we send you off in this deep village lane,
then watch earth fill your tiny grave over.

Don't say you're hardly a mile away here:
this is farewell to the very ends of heaven.

CH'*IN* SONG IN CLEAR NIGHT

The moon's risen. Birds have settled in.
Now, sitting in these empty woods, silent

mind sounding the borders of idleness,
I can tune the *ch'in*'s utter simplicities:

from the wood's nature, a cold clarity,
from a person's mind, a blank repose.

When mind's gathered clear calm *ch'i*,
wood can make such sudden song of it,

and after lingering echoes die away,
song fading into depths of autumn night,

you suddenly hear the source of change,
all heaven and earth such depths of clarity.

WINE STOPS BY FOR THE NIGHT

It's dusk, and in this west room, quiet.
I hear the *tap tap tap* out at the gate,

and knowing it's an overnight guest,
I sweep dust and dirt from the mats.

This village home has little to offer
arriving guests: a little fruit and tea,

a monk's life of poverty and silence,
four walls nestled in bamboo forests.

Kitchen lamps throw shadows outside.
The *tap* of rain under the eaves ends.

Idleness isn't great company, I know,
but why not stay and share the night?

VILLAGE SNOW, SITTING AT NIGHT

At the south window, my back to a lamp,
I sit. Wind scatters sleet into darkness.

In lone depths of silent village night:
the call of a late goose in falling snow.

THE GRAIN TAX

An officer came pounding on their gate
in the night, shouting, demanding taxes.

They didn't wait for morning. Hurrying
out to their granary, candles and lamps

alight, they winnowed grain til it shone
pure as pearls: one cart, thirty bushels.

Still they worried it wasn't fine enough,
that they'd be whipped like sorry slaves.

I once took office, a fool devoting myself
utterly, regretting my meager talents.

Paid for sitting ten years like a corpse,
I served in four different departments

and often heard old hands proclaiming:
gain and loss— it all comes round again.

If your sage hearts are so sweet and true,
why not send back a little imperial grain?

CLIMBING AMONG ANCIENT TOMBS
EAST OF THE VILLAGE

Trails of oxen and sheep overrun
all these ancient hillside tombs.

I climb to the highest mound alone,
and full of longing's raw distances,

look toward the village. Nothing
there: just grasses and waste fields.

Caring little for blossoms, villagers
keep planting chestnuts and dates.

Ever since I came back to live here
in this village, it's all felt wrong:

blossoms few, orioles rare– spring
grows old unnoticed year after year.

FOXGLOVE FARMERS

Wheat died when spring rains failed.
Early frost ravaged everything else,

so without a bite to eat at year's end,
they forage foxglove in their fields.

And what do they do with foxglove?
They barter it for a little dry grain.

Shouldering hoes out in the icy dawn,
not even a basketful when dusk turns

lean, they carry it to vermilion gates
and offer it to fair-skinned noblemen:

*If you feed some to those fine horses,
they'll glow, they'll light the ground!*

And all they ask is soured horse feed,
something to ease the pain of hunger.

VILLAGE NIGHT

Frost-covered grass silvered azure, insect song tightens.
No one north of the village, no one south of the village,

I wander out the front gate and gaze across open fields.
Moonlight shimmers, turning wheat blossoms into snow.

EYES GOING DARK

I wore myself out young, eyes bitter from long hard bookwork,
and growing old, wounded by grief, my tears seem countless.

With these ruined eyes, how will I see everything is of itself?
And once sickness takes over, what of the path to awakening?

When night falls, it's like a lamp suddenly gone dark somewhere,
and at dawn, I wonder why the mirror isn't polished and clear.

A thousand drugs, ten thousand treatments– nothing works.
What can I do but close my eyes and study that vast dharma text?

SITTING AT NIGHT

Facing the courtyard at day's end, I welcome night– that dark
realm ripe for sitting at this lamp, looking into bright clarity.

No words for such depths of heart, I wonder who can share them.
That's when the moment allows a whispered howl: once, twice.

WINTER NIGHT

Those I love scattered away, poor
and far too sick for friendly visits,

I'm shut up inside, no one in sight.
Lying in this village study alone,

the wick cold and lampflame dark,
wide open drapes torn and tattered,

I listen as the snow begins to fall
again, that hiss outside the window.

Older now, sleeping less and less,
I get up in the night and sit intent,

mind utterly forgotten. How else
can I get past such isolate silence?

Body visiting this world steadfast,
mind abandoned to change limitless:

it's been like this four years now,
one thousand three hundred nights.

WRITTEN ON A WALL AT JADE-SPRING MONASTERY

In the jade spring's clear green depths,
this body's far far off, a drifting cloud,

and a mind all idleness faces still water,
both perfect clarity, no trace of dust.

The gnarled bamboo staff's in a hand,
the silk cap on a head. Come on a whim

and gone down the mountain, the whim
vanished: can you make out who I am?

DREAMING OF LONG AGO

I've grown old since our farewell, bitterly cultivating the Tao,
refining this irreconcilable heart all the way into dead ash.

I thought I'd polished the memories of a lifetime clean away–
so how is it you came stealing into my dreams again last night?

YEN-TZU TOWER

Brilliant moonlight filling windows, frost filling blinds,
a lamp's last light flickers across the bed, the cold quilt.

A night of moonlit frost on Yen-tzu Tower: autumn's come,
but now I'm living just enough old age for one man alone.

EXILE: 815-820

READING CHUANG TZU

Leaving home and homeland, banished to some far-off place,
I wonder how it is I'm nearly free of grief and pain. Puzzled

and searching Chuang Tzu for insight on returning to dwell,
I realize it's a place beyond questions: that's our native land.

ON THE BOAT, READING YÜAN CHEN'S POEMS

I sit up with a scroll of your poems, reading before a lamp.
When I'm done, the lamp's flickering low and dawn's far off.

My eyes ache. I put out the lamp and sit in the dark. Waves
blown by headwinds: the sound of them slapping at the boat.

SETTING A MIGRANT GOOSE FREE

Snows heavy in Hsün-yang this tenth-year winter,
riverwater spawns ice, tree branches break and fall,

and hungry birds flock east and west by the hundred,
a migrant goose crying starvation loudest among them.

Pecking through snow for grass, sleeping nights on ice,
its cold wings lumber slower and slower up into flight,

and soon it's tangled in a river-boy's net, carried away
snug in his arms, and put for sale alive in the market.

Once a man of the north, I'm accused and exiled here.
Man and bird: though different, we're both visitors,

and it hurts a visiting man to see a visiting bird's pain,
so I pay the ransom and set you free. Goose, o soaring

goose rising into the clouds— where will you fly now?
Don't fly northwest: that's the last place you should go.

There in Huai-hsi, rebels still loose, there's no peace,
just a million armored soldiers long massed for battle:

imperial and rebel armies grown old facing each other.
Starved and exhausted– they'd love to get hold of you,

those tough soldiers. They'd shoot you and have a feast,
then pluck your wings clean to feather their arrows.

VISITING THE RECLUSE CHENG

Having fathomed Tao, you went to dwell among simple villages
where bamboo grows thick, opening and closing your gate alone.

This isn't a mission or pilgrimage. I've come for no real reason:
just to sit out on your south terrace and gaze at those mountains.

ON WEST TOWER

In this little town beside a vast river,
a tower teeters up, facing dusk light,

damp lowlands overgrown with green
and bottomless heavens of white dew.

I'm cut off here from my homeland.
There's nowhere to send letters home,

and news is all war in Ch'en and Ts'ai,
war still roaming on after three years.

FORTY-FIVE

I've lived through forty-five years now.
My temples half way into grizzled gray,

I'm all skin and bone and song-seized,
wine-wild and each year more abandoned

still to the inevitable unfolding of things.
Anywhere tranquil is my old home now,

and I think my thatch hut may be ready
next spring up there beside Lu Mountain.

YEAR'S END, FACING WINE AT SOUTH CREEK,
A FAREWELL TO WANG WHO'S RETURNING
TO THE CAPITAL

It's deep winter. There's ice spreading across the P'en River,
and when night comes, Lu Mountain fades into dark clouds,

snow falling, buffeted in the gusty wind and fine as rice,
scattering restless and windblown through shoreline reeds.

I've spent two years here, and this morning you start home,
sent off with a mere splash of wine. For us, facing ourselves

grown steadily older, that's plenty. It's all drifting idleness:
everything gathering and scattering, failing and succeeding.

OVERNIGHT AT EAST-FOREST MONASTERY

Through a window, lamplight gutters low.
Incense smoldering beside monks deepens.

In Lu Mountain's falling and scattering dark,
overnight at East Forest: windblown snow.

EARLY SPRING

Snow's melting, ice too letting go.
The weather mild, the wind warm,

my whole courtyard's wet and ripe,
shepherd's-purse green by the wall.

No work, no worry– it's quiet here,
dusk. In slant light, I close the gate.

I never open Chuang Tzu or Lao Tzu,
and whose company can rival theirs?

BAMBOO MOUNTAIN'S EASTERN POND

In a small pond east of Bamboo Mountain Terrace, fresh
water lilies and duckweed, a confusion of early green.

I'm a wanderer here, and taking a lamp out past midnight,
I find a pair of egrets startled away, snow-white in flight.

MY THATCH HUT NEWLY BUILT BELOW INCENSE-
BURNER PEAK, I CHANT MY THOUGHTS THEN
COPY THEM ONTO THE ROCKS

Facing Incense-Burner's north slope,
west of Yi-ai Monastery, majestic rock

outcroppings tower, stately and white,
where a clear stream tumbles and flows,

where dozens of austere pines abide
and supple bamboo a thousand strong.

Pines spreading kingfisher-blue canopies,
bamboo hung with flakes of green jade:

they've harbored no human dwelling
for who knows how many long years,

just gatherings of gibbons and birds
and mist adrift on empty wind all day.

An adept sunk in lost karma delusion,
I came here one day, a Po named Chü-i,

a man who's entire life seemed wrong,
and seeing it all, feeling mind settle

into a place that could nurture old age,
I knew at once that I would never leave,

so I framed thatch eaves against cliffs
and cleared the ravine for a tea garden.

To keep ears rinsed clean, a waterfall
washes across the roof and into flight,

and for eyes pure and clear, water lilies
drift white below a stonework terrace.

Nestling a jar of wine in my left hand
and a *ch'in's* five strings in my right,

I admire how easily contentment comes
just sitting here in the midst of all this,

and marveling at the song of heaven,
I blend in a few tipsy words and let it

voice my nature: a far-country recluse
caught in nets of human consequence.

My best years offered up day by day,
I trust old age to this mountain return,

a tired bird finding its thick forests,
a worn-out fish back in clear streams.

If I ever left here, where would I go—
that peopled realm all trial and peril?

MY THATCHED MOUNTAIN HUT JUST FINISHED, CH'I-SITED BELOW INCENSE-BURNER PEAK, I WRITE THIS ON THE EAST WALL

Three rooms and five spans– my new thatch hut boasts
stone stairs, cassia pillars and a bamboo-weave fence,

eaves lofty on the south to welcome warm winter sun,
doors and windows on the north for cool summer winds.

A waterfall sprinkling stonework dissolves into mist,
and bamboo brushing the windows grow lazy and wild.

Next spring, I'll get a side-room ready here on the east:
paper screens and cane blinds for my wife, my treasure.

ANOTHER POEM FOR THE WALL OF MY THATCH HUT

The sun's high and I've slept enough, but I'm too lazy to get up.
My hut's small, but my quilt thick. Bitter cold doesn't worry me:

propped on a pillow, I listen to the stream at Yi-ai Monastery,
and raising the blinds, I gaze at snow on Incense-Burner Peak.

Lu Mountain: it's the perfect place to get free of your name,
and a Chief Magistrate's job the perfect way to send off old age.

Mind vast and body at ease: that's where I've returned to dwell.
Now my native home's no more Ch'ang-an than anywhere else.

IDLE SONG

After such painstaking study of empty-gate dharma,
everything life plants in the mind has dissolved away:

there's nothing left now but that old poetry demon.
A little wind or moon, and I'm chanting an idle song.

AFTER LUNCH

After eating lunch, I feel so sleepy.
Waking later, I sip two bowls of tea,

then notice shadows aslant, the sun
already low in the southwest again.

Joyful people resent fleeting days.
Sad ones can't bear the slow years.

It's those with no joy and no sorrow—
they trust whatever this life brings.

ALL THE MOUNTAIN GUESTS STARTED UP
INCENSE-BURNER PEAK TOGETHER, HELPING EACH
OTHER ALONG, UNTIL RAIN FORCED US BACK
AND WE CAME HOME A DRENCHED CONFUSION
OF WILD LAUGHTER

We started climbing full of breezy serenity.
As dragon bells rang out, rain forced us back,

clinging to roots and vines on dangerous cliffs,
slipping on rocks covered with lichen and moss.

Socks a filthy mess, you poke fun at each other.
Shoes torn through, I keep laughing at myself.

Today, there really were earthen feet of mud
treading the jade staircase to celestial palaces.

REPLY TO YÜAN CHEN

You write out my poems, filling monestary walls,
and I crowd these door-screens here with yours.

Old friend, we never know where it is we'll meet—
we two duckweed leaves adrift on such vast seas.

EARLY CICADAS

On the sixth month and seventh day,
cicadas begin along the riverbank:

among thick cedars rooted in rock,
dusk going spare– two or three calls.

One hurries gray hair, and the next
carries me back to my old courtyard.

No trace of autumn or its west winds,
autumn thoughts swell, and memory

returns to the sound of scholartree
blossoms falling in palace gardens.

Dawn comes, woods above Hsün-yang
lost in mist, thoughts grown boundless.

A LATE-NIGHT FAREWELL TO MENG KUNG-TS'AO

Hsün-yang's Chief Magistrate Po offers
midnight farewells to Meng Kung-ts'ao,

the river dark, flute and string silent.
Lamps burn high in the bright tower,

billows churning the lake like arrows,
frost a knifeblade killing back grasses.

Why bother to open our writing-desks?
Shadowy winds are howling with grief.

IN THE MOUNTAINS, ASKING THE MOON

It's the same Ch'ang-an moon when I ask
which doctrine remains with us always.

It flew with me when I fled those streets,
and now shines clear in these mountains,

carrying me through autumn desolations,
waiting as I sleep away long slow nights.

If I return to my old homeland one day,
it will welcome me like family. And here,

it's a friend for strolling beneath pines
or sitting together on canyon ridgetops.

A thousand cliffs, ten thousand canyons—
it's with me everywhere, abiding always.

INVITING LIU SHIH-CHIU

Green winged-ant wine fresh and unstrained
warming over a red-clay stove. A small flame.

You've come late. Heaven's verging on snow.
You'll stay and share a cup or two, won't you?

EVENING RAIN

An early cricket sings clear, then stops.
A lamp flickers out, then flares up again.

Outside the window, telling me evening
rain's come: a clattering in banana trees.

FLOODWATERS

Once every year floodwaters sweep over
the countryside all around Hsün-yang:

gates drift away from empty villages,
towers on city walls go toppling over,

and in a land of ocean colors, boundless
kingfisher-blue blending away into sky,

wind lashes up churning whitewater
among waves the sun boils seething red.

Merchants gather their things and flee,
oxen and horses escape onto hillsides–

then the tax collector comes to plunder
what's left of farming and silk-making.

Only he can hire a boat. Each oarstroke
swelling his sense of duty, oblivious to

disaster ravaging the ten thousand people,
he's scavenging for any trace of profit.

Your resolve to end this won't last long
unless I keep urging you on: these floods

always end by autumn frostfall, leaving
the land here flat and dry, same as ever.

STILL SICK, I GET UP

It seems forever since I last stepped out my gate: I've been too sick.
And feeling stronger this morning, I doubt I'll find any company.

But a year's slipped away since I sat sipping wine on the river tower,
and spring breezes keep at me, keep fluttering those wineshop flags.

WRITTEN ON A PINE BESIDE THE STREAM AT YI-AI MONASTERY

Ancient pines grown twisted and gnarled,
rising over a stream full of tiny pebbles:

they share flowing water's quiet repose
and the towering heights of distant peaks.

If not woven into kingfisher-blue mist
or shaking off blossom-streamers of snow,

they offer monks lucid shade for sitting
and timeless cranes safe haven for rest.

How could any brush render their forms
or *ch'in* sing those harmonies so pure?

Hissing in summer wind like falling leaves,
glistening all bitter-dew on clear nights,

make them your hut. Dwell at ease here,
wandering mountain paths idle and alone:

you can't make grand roofbeams of them,
only companions deep in isolate mystery.

SUFFERING HEAT, ENJOYING COLD

Mind and body mere harried exhaustion,
I've endured the fierce heat of summer,

each day dragging on and on forever,
clear autumn always out beyond sight.

But now the harvest is over and gone,
and reaching a limit, heaven's calendar

swings back hot to cold. I watch it come,
a recluse tracing Buddha transmission:

morning's flush of heat-cloud suddenly
turning to autumn's gold wind tonight.

Pillow and mat are clear and cool now,
this body growing lighter and stronger,

so I think of friends to share the moon
and a celebration to welcome autumn.

No guests arrive. Midnight slips away,
but I keep on treating myself to wine.

EARLY CICADAS

A rising moon lights mountains first.
A sudden wind rustles lakewater first.

And it's no different for cicada song:
it fills the ears of someone idle first,

one song bringing a tangle of grief,
and the next such longing for home.

And there in Hsia-kuei, first cicada
song so long ago felt just like this.

Who was it, listening in a simple house
among scholartree blossoms at dusk?

A CH'IN AT NIGHT

Shu *t'ung*-wood true to the quick,
Ch'u silk rings out pure and clear:

harmony swelling slowly into deep
night, a scatter of sound. Listen:

pure and tasteless, a recluse mind
heartfelt calm, it appears of itself,

then returns of itself into nothing,
not the least need for human ears.

EAST TOWER BAMBOO

Cool and easy on city walls, east tower
stands nestled deep among tall bamboo:

ten thousand stalks, a forest of white
powder spreading jade-green heights.

I raise blinds, doze off. Then suddenly
seeing them, I lean on a pillow gazing

on and on, their colors filling the tower,
shadowy greens adrift on bed and mat.

Cut off from visitors in this empty city,
I face the moonlit dark alone, perfectly

alone and no plans to start back home,
invited overnight by such noble hosts.

EARLY AUTUMN

Two gray hairs appear in the lit mirror,
a single leaf tumbling into the courtyard.

Old age slips away, nothing to do with me,
and when grief comes, who does it find?

Idle months and years emptying away,
loved ones from long ago lost to sight,

I'll play with my girl here, my little girl:
we keep coaxing smiles from each other.

WINTER SUN ON MY BACK

A winter sun rises huge and bright,
lights the south corner of my house.

Eyes closed, I sit warming my back,
ch'i stirring through every muscle,

serene. Soon it's like sipping wine,
like the refreshment of hibernation.

Body genial, its hundred bones clear,
spirit serene, no thoughts anywhere,

I've forgotten where I am, boundless
mind all emptiness rendered whole.

THE PA RIVER

Below the city, where the Pa River's water flows,
spring comes like yeast-powder spiriting wine:

beaches feel soft as the Wei's meandering shores,
and cliffs bring memories of T'ien-chin Bridge,

but fresh yellow willows dip their shadows here,
and tiny white duckweed blossoms scent the air.

Sitting beside swelling water, I scratch my head:
all this grief and sorrow, and whose is it anyway?

NIGHT OF THE COLD FOOD FESTIVAL

It's my forty-ninth year now, and even the sun looks old and worn.
Tonight's the hundred and fifth, a moon lighting up all heaven.

I clutch my knees, sit and brood, wondering what it's all come to,
when suddenly a silly girl and loony boy are calling me out to swing!

PLANTING EAST SLOPE

I took money to buy flowering trees,
planted them on the city's east slope:

not just peach and apricot and plum,
I bought everything that would bloom,

planted hundreds in such confusion,
blossoms everywhere in their season,

heaven bringing them early and late,
earth fostering high and low together.

Reds are clouds so flushed and radiant
and whites snow so pure and bright

wandering bees can't bear to leave,
and lovely birds flock here to roost.

There's an endless stream facing them
and a small level terrace down below

where I often sweep the stones clean
then raise a cup of wine to the wind.

Branches in bloom shading my head,
blossom-dust scattered across my chest,

I'm alone– drinking, chanting poems,
oblivious to a sun sinking in the west.

Adoring blossoms isn't a tradition here.
Spring ends, and no one's come gazing,

no one but the exalted Prefect. Drunk
all day, he just can't tear himself away.

REPLY IN THE SAME RHYME TO A QUATRAIN SENT BY CH'IEN HUI

Adepts to the emperor of emptiness, our months and years deepen,
and thinking of each other so far away, we send chanted *samādhi*:

inhabiting the quiet and remote clarity abiding always in change,
there's nothing to it but diamond-pure, diamond-hard sutra mind.

MIDDLE POEMS: 820-829

TRAVELING MOON

A traveler from those southlands,
I set out as a crescent moon rose.

In a journey all distances, I saw
clear moonlight three times full,

trailed an old moon away at dawn,
then met a new one for the night.

Who says the moon is heartless?
It's followed me a thousand miles.

Leaving a Wei River bridge early,
I'm in Ch'ang-an streets by dusk,

but this moon keeps on traveling,
stays the night who knows where.

MY OLD HOME

Below distant walls, crickets weave autumn song. Tender gaze
drifting low, the moon casts fresh shadows in under the eaves.

The bed-curtains are old, ribbons gracing blinds broken short,
and now the cold comes before evening dark starts settling in.

ENJOYING PINE AND BAMBOO

1

Dragons and snakes haunt marshlands
while paired deer roam thick grasslands,

phoenixes live content in *wu-tung* trees
while hermit fish delight in duckweed–

and I'm just like them, in love with my
thatch hut, my simple ways pure delight.

Pines out front, bamboo lofty in back,
I could idle away old age with ease here.

Everything stays close to what keeps it
content, no idea what others may crave.

2

I treasure what front eaves face
and all that north windows frame.

Bamboo winds lavish out windows,
pine colors exquisite beyond eaves,

I gather it all into isolate mystery,
thoughts fading into their source.

Others may feel nothing in all this,
but it's perfectly open to me now:

such kindred natures need share
neither root nor form nor gesture.

A GUEST DOESN'T COME

Candleflame red and wine clear, I settle in and just wait.
At dawn's first light, I'm wandering in and out the gate,

stars thin and moon drifting low. No guest. Night's now
sunrise lost in willow mist, a magpie taking flight, gone.

BOUNDLESS AND FREE

I'll never adore this body again,
never loathe it again. How is it

worth adoring when it brings
ten thousand kalpas of trouble,

or loathing when it's emptiness
clumped together in empty dust?

Done adoring it, done loathing it:
so we begin boundless and free.

ON SHANG MOUNTAIN ROAD

I'd been summoned back. I remember a day—
the three of us on this road home together . . . .

It's all a dream— this life of ours, everything
slipping into the past, returning to emptiness.

Li Chien a burial-jade in the nethersprings,
Ts'ui Shao a breeze among mourning candles,

I'm the only one left now: old remnant Chü-i,
hair white, heading back beyond the Yangtze.

FIGURES FOR A MONK

Kalpa winds drive flames that rage through deserted homes.
Oceans of misery churn broken boats on vast seething swells.

Weak, no need for rescue from the ravages of fire and water,
you sit at peace, plumb *ch'an* beneath Cold-Clarity Mountain.

AUTUMN BUTTERFLIES

Blossoms a deep maroon haze, autumn
butterflies appear everywhere: teeming

yellow flecks, they hang from blossoms,
frolic in crowded flight east and west.

At nightfall, when the cold winds come,
a confusion of crowded blossoms falls,

and in the depths of night, dew ice-cold,
butterflies fill out the crowds of death.

It's true of all things kindred in *ch'i*:
born this morning, dead tonight. No one

sees thousand-year immortality cranes:
they perch high in thousand-foot pines.

OVERNIGHT AT BAMBOO PAVILION

Sit through dusk beneath eaves of pine
at Bamboo Pavilion, sleep night away:

it's such empty clarity, like some drug,
isolate mystery deep as a mountain home.

No cleverness can rival a simple mind,
and industry never outshines idleness.

Done struggling, done cultivating Tao:
here it is, this remote DarkEnigma gate.

FLOWER NO FLOWER

Flower no flower
mist no mist

arrives at midnight
and leaves at dawn

arrives like a spring dream– how many times
leaves like a morning cloud– nowhere to find.

FOR THE BEACH GULLS

The crush of age is turning my hair white
and I'm stuck with purple robes of office,

but if my body's tangled in these fetters,
my heart abides where nothing's begun.

Happening on wine, I'm drunk in no time,
and loving those mountains, I return late.

They don't know who I am. Seeing official
falcon-banners flutter, beach gulls scatter.

A SIGH FOR MYSELF

At dawn, my gray hair falling out, I'm lazy with the comb,
and in spring, eyes growing dim, I'm quick to burn herbs.

There isn't much left to me now. I just wander, all idleness
lost to the things people feel, hardly even human anymore.

UP EARLY

Sunrise flares in my room, roofbeams ablaze, incandescent.
Somewhere a door opens: and it's a booming drum sounded once.

Our dog's asleep on the stairs, meaning a rain-soaked earth,
but birds chattering at the window tell me about clear skies.

Last night's wine not yet thinned away, my head feels heavy,
and no longer wearing winter clothes, my body's light again.

Dozing off, it's clear how empty mind is, how thought expires.
Even dreams of home– these days they rarely go all the way.

OVERNIGHT AT BAMBOO TOWER

For simple books, a thousand bamboo below the tower,
and for bottomless flame, a single lamp before the stove . . . .

Who is there kindred enough to share all this tonight–
pure-fire monk, master of Tao's alchemy sitting *ch'an?*

FAREWELL TO MY DAY LILIES AND CASSIA

No longer Prefect, this isn't home anymore.
I planted day lilies and cassia for nothing.

Cassia renowned for enticing us to stay on,
day-lillies never making it *sorrow forgotten:*

they're a far cry from this riverside moon,
come lingering out farewell step after step.

LI THE MOUNTAIN RECLUSE STAYS THE NIGHT ON OUR BOAT

It's dusk, my boat such tranquil silence,
mist rising over waters deep and still,

and to welcome a guest for the night,
there's evening wine, an autumn *ch'in*.

A master at the gate of Tao, my visitor
arrives from exalted mountain peaks,

lofty cloudswept face raised all delight,
heart all sage clarity spacious and free.

Our thoughts begin where words end.
Refining DarkEnigma depths, we gaze

quiet mystery into each other and smile,
sharing the mind that's forgotten mind.

RISING LATE

Birds are calling in courtyard trees
and sunlight's bright in the eaves,

but I'm old, my laziness perfected,
and now it's cold I rise even later.

It's my nature: quilts thick or thin,
pillows high or low. They suit me:

spirit at peace, body safe and warm.
How many can savor such things?

Once I've slept enough, I just sit
looking up, no thoughts anywhere–

as if our senses had never opened
and our limbs were long forgotten.

I think back to someone up early
in Ch'ang-an, clothes frost-stained.

He and I, each whole and sufficient–
who can say which is nothing now?

CH'IN

Letting my *ch'in* stay on its little table,
I sit idly, letting what I feel stay deep.

Why bother to play it? In this breeze,
strings sing perfectly well themselves.

BESIDE THE POND, UNDER BAMBOO

A path winds past brambleweave fence and simple home,
jade-green: ten acres of idle dwelling, a pond gracing half.

After eating my fill and dozing refreshed at the window,
I wander off under the trees, alone, my feet light as air,

for water clarifies the spirit no less than a perfect friend,
and bamboo is a master that frees the mind to emptiness.

Why worry about that world of people, why plague mind
and ruin eyes in search of a kindred spirit here or there?

NIGHT IN THE CITY, LISTENING TO LI THE MOUNTAIN RECLUSE PLAY *THREE JOYS*

Unsheathed, a *ch'in* takes to autumn
wind, moonlit doors open to night.

Sounding Master Jung Ch'i's deep joys,
this Su-chou Prefect utter idleness,

you distill in a moment of thought
a thousand ancient forevers gone,

and I'm just another Chung Tzu-ch'i:
all I hear are rivers and mountains.

FIRST MONTH, THIRD DAY: AN IDLE STROLL

At Golden-Oriole Lane, orioles are just beginning to sing,
and at Crow-and-Magpie Stream, ice is beginning to thaw.

Water stretches away everywhere, swells all emerald green,
three-hundred-ninety bridges flaunting crimson handrails,

and ducks drift in pairs, wings close and ripples mingling,
where willows weave their branches together by the million.

There's no asking whether spring winds come early or late:
they arrive in the morning where yesterday becomes today.

A SIGH FOR MYSELF

Old age isn't the only thing to endure.
I'm beseiged too by all this sickness:

asthma starting up again each spring,
cough going deeper every year, eyes

darker. But I can see to brush and ink.
My hair's white, but hairpins stay put.

And isn't following days and months
away where I found this simple heart?

TWO STONES

These two scraps of stone dusky azure,
looking so utterly gnarled and strange:

they're useless for anything practical
so no one's ever bothered with them.

After taking shape in embryonic mud,
emerging from Tung-t'ing Lake to drift

shorelines through boundless antiquity,
they came into my hands one morning.

Hauling them inside, I scrubbed them
clean, rinsed away dirt and mud to find

smoky scars veined into dark hollows,
mossy greens thick in splintered blues,

and seeing feet of old coiling dragons
amid hefts of ancient swords sunk deep,

things so far from this human realm,
I start thinking they fell from heaven.

One's the perfect place to leave a *ch'in*,
and the other just right to store wine

(one a little cragged peak towering up,
the other hollow enough for a quart),

so I'll prop my five-string on the left
and let my winecup perch on the right,

for wine ladled out won't empty the pool,
and jade mountain slopes never change.

People all harbor their special loves,
and things all seek their kindred spirits,

but I'm afraid in their childhood fields
they never saw white-haired old men.

Turning my head, I ask these two stones
if an old-timer could ever be their friend,

and though they can't speak, my stones
both promise we are indeed friends three.

SIXTH MONTH, THIRD DAY: LISTENING
TO CICADAS AT NIGHT

Clear frost opening water-lily scents,
a lovely wind starts willows rustling.

A thin moon rises into its third night,
then first cicada song starts drifting,

and hearing it, a visitor growing sad,
I listen quietly, thinking of Lo-yang:

at my home there among the bamboo,
cicadas have sung again since I left.

I don't know: this pond of moonlight,
and whoever set this little boat adrift?

OVERNIGHT IN THE UPPER COURTYARD OF
LING-YEN MONASTERY

An incandescent moon rising, soaring high over green forests,
guests gone and monks back inside, the lone night grows deep.

I've given up meals of flesh and blood, traded them for wine,
and all those bells and songs fading away, I keep my *ch'in* close.

You won't find the world's tawdry affairs crowding your eyes
here. Here, the rippling sounds of a stream rinse mind clean,

and looking east from the morning terrace, it's beyond compare:
in T'ai Lake's misty water, the greens are bottomless, bottomless.

OVERNIGHT AT JUNG-YANG

I was born and raised here in Jung-yang,
but left its village paths young. And now,

after forty years and so many distances,
I've come back again for another night.

When we left, I was only eleven or twelve,
and here I am, turned fifty-six this year,

thinking back to boyhood days, to games
we played. I can still see it all so clearly,

but the neighborhood I once called home:
it's gone now, and my old family vanished.

And it isn't just the village that's changed,
the very hills and valleys are transformed:

there's nothing left but the Ch'en and Wei,
rivers flowing heartless and green as ever.

IDLE SONG

In moonlight, I envied vistas of clarity,
and in pine sleep adored green shadow.

I wrote grief-torn poems when young,
plumbed the depths of feeling when old.

Now I sit up all night practicing *ch'an*,
and autumn can still bring a sudden sigh,

but that's it. Two last ties. Beyond them,
nothing anywhere holds this mind back.

LIVING IDLY IN THE HSIN-CH'ANG DISTRICT, I INVITE YANG JU-SHIH'S BROTHERS TO VISIT

A sick old man, cap gauze and pillow horn, I doze.
Never in haste, always in idleness: who's like me,

who but these two pines at the bottom of the steps,
their minds never touched by tangles and worries?

Golden seals and purple ribbons are a dream now,
black canopies and red wheels emptiness forgotten.

In this midsummer heat, what can my simple home
offer a visitor? Just a breeze at the north window.

ON LING-YING TOWER, LOOKING NORTH

This high up, I begin to see how small our human realm is,
face distances and know the kingdom of perception is pure

emptiness. Turning away, I start home through the morning
markets– a kernel of darnel tumbling into the vast granary.

SITTING IDLE AT THE NORTH WINDOW

The window empty: two thickets of bamboo.
The house tranquil: a single fragrant stove.

Beyond the gate, it's red dust everywhere,
and in the city, that white sun hurries on,

but I don't chase after immortality masters,
don't long for the arts of everlasting life.

I have my own secret for stretching it out:
when the mind's idle, months and years last.

QUIET DWELLING DURING THE SECLUSION FAST

Sickness comes, but the mind's quiet: not a single thought.
Old age passes, but my body's idle: who lives to a hundred?

I've forgotten the dust that crowds eyes, adore only sleep,
but little by little, my word-karma keeps spawning poems.

Dwelling here, free of meat through this month of fasting,
incense flame is my constant companion. I sit tranquil–

ten thousand worries and the hundred gods in exhaltation
gone, nothing but the silence that ends our three spirits.

BLOSSOMS FOR A MONK'S COURTYARD

To realize the emptiness of appearance, that is the Buddhist pursuit,
and so I've planted this flowering tree here at your monk's home.

If you look closely, it's no different than the *Flower-Garland Sutra*,
and so handy: A little wind opens perfect *prajñā*-wisdom blossoms.

FACING WINE

Insisting on clever or stupid, sage or fool, *yes this* and *no that:*
it's nothing like wine. Drunk, you forget clean back to the very

origin of things, fathom the expanse of all heaven and earth,
a phoenix or eagle lofting itself out into flight and soaring free.

LATE POEMS: 829-846

AUTUMN POOL

My body's idle, doing perfectly nothing,
and mind, thinking perfectly nothing,

now more than ever. In this old garden
tonight, I've returned to my autumn pool,

shoreline dark now birds have settled in,
bridge incandescent under a rising moon.

Chestnut scents swell, adrift on a breeze,
and the cinnamon's a confusion of lit dew.

So much solitude in this far end of quiet,
an isolate mystery no one finally knows:

just a few words haunting a far-off mind,
asking why it took so long coming here.

LÜ-TAO DISTRICT, DWELLING IN SPRING

Sparse rain sprinkles garden trees, then
a clearing, lovely, lights a patch of leaves,

and below, wind rinses across pond water,
slant light splitting blossoms to the core.

Here, nightfall thickens shadows in mist,
and spring deepens water's depth of color.

I'm not like T'ao Ch'ien: for enlightenment,
I like to keep my *ch'in* thoroughly strung.

MEETING AN OLD FRIEND

Suddenly meeting again after so long,
we're convinced it must be a dream.

Happening upon such joy, we let go,
pour wine, perfect all this emptiness.

LONG LINES SENT TO LING HU-CH'U BEFORE HE
COMES TO VISIT MY TUMBLEDOWN HOME

No esteem for the stately caps and carriages of consequence,
in love with woods and streams, I go out and doze, perhaps,

drunk beside the pond. I've stopped trying to save the world,
just wander herb paths, keep my little fishing boat swept out.

Serving the poetry master with writing-brush and inkstone,
I'm steadied by music and my friend, the immortality in wine,

but for lofty sentiments, I stay close to things themselves:
green moss, rock bamboo-shoots, water lilies in white bloom.

IDLE SONG

Just another day slipping away all idleness,
nothing anywhere to tangle me in worry,

I sleep mornings with guests up and about,
and lunch at noon while monk friends fast.

Shadow gathering in trees reaches the door,
the pond spreads water right up to the stairs,

and gracing depths of night, a windswept
moon's come from long-ago Yangtze or Huai.

NEW YEAR'S EVE

Eyes sick– I don't sleep, don't join the New Year's celebrations,
and now, this heart already glutted with feeling, I face spring.

The guttering lamp's burned itself out and morning light comes
simple enough: just a sixty-year-old man, head calm and clear.

OFF-HAND CHANT

All the clothes and food I'll need here before me,
the mind free of all happiness, free of all sadness:

it's like some kind of afterlife. So what do you do
when you want nothing from this human world?

Eyes closed, I read Taoist classics in silent depths,
and this idle, I hardly bow greeting Ch'an guests.

Luckily residue remains: a cloud and stream joy.
Every year I wander Lung-men hills a few times.

THE WEST WIND

The west wind just began a few days ago,
and already the first leaves have flown.

Skies clearing anew, I dawn slight clogs
and clothes thick against this first chill,

channels rinsing thin water slowly away,
sparse bamboo a last trickle of slant light.

Soon, in a lane of green moss, dusk spare,
a servant-boy comes leading cranes home.

RISING LATE

I've slept away morning's lavish luster.
Rising as nightfall ends day, yawning,

I quickly light a warm fire in the stove,
linger long gazing into a chill mirror,

then melt snow and make a fragrant tea,
whip up curds and cook cream pudding.

Lazy and insatiable both, I just laugh:
who could understand this zest for life?

My wine's boundless, and no side-effects,
my *ch'in* simplicity pure and grief-free,

and those three noble-minded joys offer
nothing like kid-games with a baby boy.

THE POND WEST OF MY OFFICE

Not yet *ch'i*-infused, willow branches heave and sway,
and just now clear of ice, the pond ripples and swells.

Today it seems a plan perfect beyond all accounting:
spring wind and spring waters come this same moment.

HOME GROUND

Wondering where home ground is for this body and mind,
why think only of Ch'ang-an or Lo-yang and nowhere else

when I've made a career of water and bamboo and blossom,
found my home village among *ch'in* and poem and wine?

Did Master Jung-ch'i refuse deep joy when old age came?
And was Chieh Yü's song ever anything but wild and crazy?

Why squander gold on a perfect village home, when here
east of town, owned by no one, there's all this spring light?

MOURNING A-TS'UI

A three-year-old son, lone pearl treasured so in the hand.
A sixty-year-old father, hair a thousand streaks of snow,

I can't think through it– you become some strange thing,
and sorrow endless now you'll never grow into a person.

There's no swordstroke clarity when grief tears the heart,
and tears darkening my eyes aren't rinsing red dust away,

but I'm still nurturing emptiness– emptiness of heaven's
black black, this childless life stretching away before me.

POND, WINDOW

Evening pond: water lily scents drift away.
Autumn window: bamboo thoughts deepen.

For friendship here, there's no one left now.
I face a single strung *ch'in*– and just stay.

THINKING OF TS'UI HSÜAN-LIANG

Wandering mountains, following rivers, opening a scroll of poems,
gazing at moons, searching out blossoms, raising a cupful of wine:

six pursuits that defy all thought when we share them, my friend.
How long now before you come back to your Lo-yang home again?

IDLE NIGHT

An early cicada's single note drifts.
A few new fireflies flicker through.

No mist. Incense lamps burn clear,
bamboo skins all dew-stained clarity.

Still not going back inside to sleep,
I take the steps out front: moonlight

slanting deep under the porch roof,
a cold wind filling treetop heights.

Left to themselves, thoughts at ease
see through appearances they love,

and what law explains such a thing?
In the mind realm, nothing's trifling.

A SERVANT GIRL IS MISSING

From the low walls of our small courtyard
to the notice-board outside our district gate,

I've searched and searched, ashamed our love
proved meager, wishing I could do it all over.

But a caged bird can't bear a master for long,
and the branch means nothing to a blossom

freed on the wind. Where can she be tonight?
Only the moon's understanding light knows.

MY FIRST VISIT TO INCENSE-MOUNTAIN MONASTERY, FACING THE MOON

Here at Incense Mountain, already old, I walk out into night
for the first time, meet autumn's first pellucid round of moon.

Thinking this, this is surely my home-mountain moon now,
I try asking such radiant clarity if it might feel the same way.

IN REPLY TO *AUTUMN NIGHT, NO SLEEP*, SENT
BY LIU YÜ-HSI

Bamboo emerald green, gauze curtains maroon,
the night's cold and the wind-rinsed landscape

clear here. Sick, I feel the healing *ch'i* of herbs,
and thirsty, I hear tea-cake rolled into powder.

Dew-frosted bamboo plunders lamplight shadow.
Mist-filled pines shelter moonlight's radiance.

How can there be a thousand miles between us?
Our autumn thoughts arise out of one moment.

AT THE POND, A FAREWELL

Starry array adrift all night, ShimmerWords meets the sun's return.
This is the hour when clouds wandering Lo Stream thin and scatter,

phoenix and egret rising into heaven, and blossoms chase currents
away, away– no reason to gather again at a pond beside Chü-i's home.

ASKING THE ROCK THAT HOLDS UP MY CH'IN

A star falling, thinking the whole sky must be coming down too,
you could only mourn that burial in mud beneath a deep stream.

Here on earth it's nothing like life in heaven's constant array,
After holding up a loom of origins there, what's this *ch'in* to you?

But when I wipe you clean, full of affection, do you understand?
You say nothing, so it's clear enough we share a kindred mind.

IN ANSWER TO A LETTER SENT BY LIU YÜ-HSI
ON AN AUTUMN DAY

Grateful to escape such grave illness,
I'm happy to wither away at the root,

let this lamp gauge darkening eyes,
my belt measure this thinning waist.

On a day of frost turning leaves red,
in a time of hair gone white as snow,

I may grieve over old age coming on.
But once old age ends, I'm grief-free.

EARLY MORNING, TAKING CLOUD-MOTHER POWDER

I take cloud-petal powder at dawn, then spend the day drawing water
and bathing my mouth, feeling lost in some silence of mist and haze.

When the medicine thins away, it's dusk. I try a few spoonfuls of rice,
and thirsty for wine in all these depths of spring, sip at a bowl of tea.

Every night I sit in ch'an stillness, gazing into pondwater and moon,
and sometimes I wander drunk, playing games with blossom and wind.

Abiding in the pattern inherent to things, your name rinsed clean—
who could ever explain it: body always home, mind always setting out?

AT THE POND, AN IDLE CHANT

Not a village or recluse home, or a monk's retreat either,
it's just ten acres: pond and pavilion, trees and bamboo.

Not a Taoist or Ch'an monk, or a common official either,
I dwell behind closed gates in plain robes and crow cap,

aimless thoughts wandering dreams, like some butterfly,
life all idleness and mind joy, no different from any fish.

And I still can't decide between life and death for certain:
where's the winning among them, and where the losing?

OVERNIGHT WITH CH'AN MASTER SHEN CHAO

The year's third moon old and dark,
blossoms crowd the mountain pears.

At Lung-men's Shui-hsi Monastery
we meet tonight, this Hui Yüan and I,

and sit late, facing ourselves together,
whispers intricate beyond knowing:

a place past and future lose all limits,
a time where thoughts never began.

AFTER *QUIET JOYS AT SOUTH GARDEN*, WHICH
P'EI TU SENT

This hut isolate and clear beside the pond:
surely this is what lofty thoughts must be,

blinds in the occassional breeze stirring,
a bridge shining late sun back into water.

I've grown quiet here, company to cranes,
and so idle I'm like any other cloud adrift.

Why bother to go study under Duke Liu
or search wild peaks for Master Red Pine?

READING CH'AN SUTRAS

In all the difference appearance reveals, there's no difference,
and even dwelling beyond any trace of residue is itself residue.

Forget words in the midst of words, and you see through it all.
Root out dream in the midst of dream, and you double absence.

But how can you harvest fruit from the blossom of emptiness,
and how can you catch a meal of fish in some lakewater mirage?

To still relentless change is Ch'an, and Ch'an is change itself.
No Ch'an and no change– there lies what seems in what seems.

NIGHTFALL AT SOUTH POND

It is dusk. White pondwater holds its color
as bright clouds slowly fade into darkness,

then wind shatters water lilies into fans,
ripples jostling moon into a pearl scrim.

Crickets sing out, calling back and forth.
Ducks cluster into pairs to pass the night.

A little boy hurries to announce nightfall
and returns, footsteps still a little unsure.

SITTING ALONE IN MY LITTLE THATCHED PAVILION AFTER ILLNESS, AN INVITATION FOR LI SHEN

No guests yet for my new pavilion,
alone at day's end, what shall I do?

It's warm, so I enamel the tea-stove,
weave the fence tight against cold,

and now the headaches have eased
my eyes of darkness seem brighter,

so I ladle out wine, a third of a cup,
and idly write some lines on a wall.

Then it's time to set out two chairs,
one of which awaits you even now.

ON CLIMBING THE TOWER AT T'IEN-KUAN MONASTERY WITH HUANG-FU SHU EARLY ONE AUTUMN MORNING, THOUGHTS RHYMED SIX TIMES

Azure heaven suddenly bottomless clarity
beginning another day bright and long,

this tower shimmers with morning light,
autumn pipes and strings clear and pure.

Chang Han deepening wine past renown,
Chi K'ang passing his days in idleness . . . .

Grief-tangles crowding this world of dust
thin away beyond the clouds, and knowing

how woodcutters leave a sick tree in peace,
how fetters can't snarl a deep-sky goose,

a few masters wander boundless and free,
always glad for companions in idleness.

WAVES SIFTING SAND

1

One anchorage of sand appears as another dissolves away,
and one fold of wave ends as another rises. Wave and sand

mingling together day after day, sifting through each other
without cease: they level up mountains and seas in no time.

2

White waves swell through wide open seas, boundless and beyond,
and level sands stretch into the four directions all endless depths:

evenings they dissolve and mornings reappear, sifting ever away,
their seasons transforming eastern seas into a field of mulberries.

3

Ten thousand miles across a lake where the grass never fades,
a lone traveler, you find yourself in rain among yellow plums,

gazing grief-stricken toward an anchorage of sand. Dark waves
wind keeps churned up: the sound of them slapping at the boat.

5

A day will no doubt come when dust flies at the bottom of seas,
and how can mountaintops avoid the transformation to gravel?

Young lovers may part, a man leaving, setting out on some boat,
but who could say they'll never come together again one day?

WRITTEN ON SUNG MOUNTAIN'S EASTERN CLIFFS IN EARLY SPRING

Skies clearing above thirty-six peaks,
kingfisher-blue mists rise over snowmelt.

The moon's drifted through three nights
now, spring opening across four mountains:

grasses turning distances an early green
while cold birds leave silence unchanged.

Here below the highest of these east cliffs:
nothing but a name I've scrawled on rock.

OLD, AND A FEVER

I eat up, the hundred feelings vanish,
sip wine, ten thousand worries end,

and knowing we're all ravaged by age
I've grown old without all that worry.

Scholars devoting themselves to office,
farmers struggling out in their fields:

how many escape the fevers of grief?
But having only a fever of the body,

I can lie in wind at the north window
or sit beside south pond in moonlight,

take off my crow cap, sun a cold head,
or bathe feverish feet in clear water.

Passing lazy days propped on pillows,
I rise late, drift nights away in a boat,

come into all this contentment simply
because I've stopped longing for more.

Ask friends and family about Chü-i,
ask if it's true or not. They'll tell you.

But I'm still not free of words, these
lines full of heaven vast and distant,

vast and distant beyond your knowing
here in such depths of isolate mystery.

That's my fear: you might understand
and hurry here to wander beside me.

AUTUMN RAIN, A NIGHT OF SLEEP

It's a late autumn night, cold and quiet.
A lone old man at ease here in idleness,

I lie down late, after the lamp goes dark,
sleep deep and rich amid sounds of rain.

Ashes burn all night under the winejar,
and incense keeps the quilt-rack warm.

Day dawns cold and clear, but I stay put.
Frosty leaves crowd the steps with red.

SIXTY-SIX

Sickness reveals a mind weakening,
and age the rush of light and shadow.

I came back home here at fifty-eight,
and now I've already turned sixty-six:

hair a million bleached-silk streaks,
pond grass eight or nine times green.

Children suddenly full-grown people
and garden thickets mostly tall trees,

I gaze off high rocks into mountains,
trace streams back to bamboo depths,

never getting enough of this, at least,
this rippling sound of water flowing.

GROWN-OLD SONG, SENT TO LIU YÜ-HSI

Grown this old, both of us together,
I still wonder what it's like to be old.

Eyes congested, I'm the first to bed.
At dawn, head lazy, I skip the comb.

Sometimes out with a walking-stick,
sometimes home in idleness all day,

I'm too careless for polished mirrors
and never read books in small print.

My love for old lost friends thickens
while memories of youth thin away:

there's nothing left but this idle talk,
enough and more for your next visit.

COOL AUTUMN, IDLE DOZING

Summer heat lingering on, days long:
autumn's young. These cool mornings,

water lilies set clear dew-scents adrift,
gossamer rhyme filling breezy bamboo.

Old and sick, I've dozed all day in idle
mystery, no one come asking after me:

before the gate here, dusk gone spare,
scholartree blossoms lie a full inch deep.

FACING WINE ON A WINTER'S NIGHT, SENT TO HUANG-FU SHIH

Frost killed everything in the courtyard.
Ice spreads on the pond behind my house,

and wind keeps shaking the trees, empty
and futile: no leaves to abandon branches.

It's the tenth month, night long and bitter
deep into the second half of my hundred

years in life. A fresh winejar open, I sit:
no thoughts, no heart left for any of this.

AN OLD SU-CHOU PREFECT

An old Prefect come so long ago from south of the Yangtze—
who would recognize me now, sitting here beside this pond?

It isn't just my hair turned to snow. Those pellucid Su-chou
cranes are dead, those white water lilies withered and gone.

POEMS IN SICKNESS

1. WIND SICKNESS STRIKES

I'm 68 now, feeble and frail, besieged
feeble and frail by a hundred diseases,

but a rotting tree never avoids grubs,
and wind finds empty hollows with ease.

Fingers may be numb as willow shoots,
head tumbling, dizzy as brambleblow,

but there's this place, dead-still serene,
this heart gone blank and white as sky.

2. LYING IN BED

Winds of disease have stolen into my old head, cold enough
blood stiffens and muscles congeal, nothing of me at ease,

but I don't mind living out my life in these isolate distances,
trusting myself to the past, that lavish shimmer wandering

lost. Thinking back on what's past, it's a confusion of dream,
and looking ahead my life's all dark mystery drifting free,

but when the ch'i-flood itself fills a room of ch'an stillness,
how could a sudden galestorm ever disturb this empty boat?

When my stomach's empty, I begin with pine-flower wine;
knees cold, I wrap them in layers of cinnamon-cloth quilts.

People may wonder whether such sickness has me worried,
but isn't this where the inevitable unfolding of things leads?

4. QUATRAINS IN SICKNESS

Birth soon becomes old age, and then old age sickness.
I've understood all this, held it in mind forever now:

at this point, the years of my life verging on seventy,
I should be ashamed this illness was so late in coming.

My heart's turned to ash and my hair to bleached silk:
even if I were still strong, what good would it do me?

No longer tangled in the worries of family and career,
I live idle and serene: what a perfect time for sickness.

9. FAREWELL TO A SUNG MOUNTAIN TRAVELER

No more climbing peaks for me, no more following streams—
so who abides there, part of rock and stream, mist and cloud?

When you reach the sunlit south exposure of Sung, sing out
these lines, chant them until its thirty-six peaks understand.

SICK AND OLD, SAME AS EVER: A POEM TO FIGURE IT ALL OUT

Splendor and ruin, sorrow and joy, long life or early death:
when this human realm's a figment of prank and whimsy,

is it really so strange if I'm soon a bug's arm or rat's liver?
And chicken skin or crane plumage– what would it hurt?

In yesterday's winds, I was happy to begin my long journey,
but today, in all this sunlit warmth of spring, I feel better.

And now that I'm packed and ready for that distant voyage,
what does it matter if I linger on a little while longer here?

IN THE MOUNTAINS

It will come: the great transformation of seas to mulberry fields.
Heaven and earth seething, all wind-churned swells and billows,

feasting whales and battling dragons will turn the waves to blood.
But what do these fish know, happily wandering a deep stream?

AT HOME GIVING UP HOME

There's plenty of food and clothes. The children are married.
Now that I'm free and clear of all those duties to the family,

I fall asleep at night with the body of a bird reaching forests
and eat at dawn with the mind of a monk who begs for meals.

A scatter of crystalline voices calls: cranes beneath pines.
A single fleck of cold light burns: a lamp in among bamboo.

On a sitting cushion, I'm all *ch'an* stillness deep in the night.
A daughter calls, a wife hoots: no answer, no answer at all.

DWELLING IN IDLENESS

Isolate autumn silence, all wind and rain and visitors rare,
the gate stays closed all day and the courtyard cold and quiet,

my white horse with its black mane and gold bridle just sold
and WillowBranch with her gossamer sleeves gone back home.

I can browse through book-scrolls when I want some sleep,
and sipping at a splash of wine still starts me smiling a little,

but my eyes are darkness, so I walk out into moonless nights,
and such swollen feet mean no mountains climbed in spring.

A mind of silence can't keep stillness from this noisy place.
The impulse of change forgotten, it's all a dream of idleness

where *yes this* and *no that,* love and hate have vanished into
thin air. Nothing left– just an empty life I trust to this world.

COLD NIGHT

Pellucid dew and crystalline wind, the courtyard gate cold,
an old man keeping warm in lined robes this first icy night.

Dancing waists and singing sleeves: where have they gone?
Just me and the enlightenment of a single stringless *ch'in*.

FACING ROCKS I PLACED IN YI-CHÜ STREAM
TO BREAK UP THE CURRENT NEAR THE WALL
WEST OF MY THATCHED PAVILION, I COME
TO HARMONIES OF TUMBLING WATER AND
THE HINT OF ISOLATE MYSTERY

These rocks cragged Sung Mountain
cliffs in the Yi-chü's moonlit clarity:

majestic as distant peaks, they exact
sounds of cold jade from the stream.

Gossamer trees crowding the banks,
I open my little pavilion, sit facing

whitewater, sure the Yen-tzu River's
tumbling here through Lo-yang City.

This is when things settle in to rest.
Wind silent, a subtle moon lighting

spacious quiet, I let all these autumn
clarities brim full through my ears.

All day long abiding in the great Tao:
who can understand such heartfelt

depths, depths so ample and composed
they don't care if anyone ever hears?

COLD PAVILION: AN INVITATION

It's morning and I'm sitting all idleness in my rock pavilion,
flames in the stove fallen into embers, winecup still empty.

The cold's arranged its scatterings here, as if inviting guests:
ice-covered pond, frost-stained bamboo, old man hair of snow.

THE NORTH WINDOW: BAMBOO AND ROCK

A majesterial rock windswept and pure
and a few bamboo so lavish and green:

facing me, they seem full of sincerity.
I gaze into them and can't get enough,

and there's more at the north window
and along the path beside West Pond:

wind sowing bamboo clarities aplenty,
rain gracing the subtle greens of moss.

My wife's still here, frail and old as me,
but no one else: the children are gone.

Leave the window open. If you close it,
who'll keep us company for the night?

CLIMBING MOUNTAINS IN DREAM

Nights hiking Sung Mountain in dream,
just a goosefoot walking-stick and me:

a thousand cliffs, ten thousand canyons,
I wander until I've explored them all,

my stride in dream as it was in youth,
strong and sure and so free of disease.

When I wake, spirit become itself again
and body returned to flesh and blood,

I realize that in terms of body and spirit,
body grows sick while spirit's immune,

and yet body and spirit are both mirage,
dream and waking merest appearance.

Scarcely able to hobble around by day
then roaming free all night with ease:

in the equal division of day and night
what have I ever gained and what lost?

TO GET OVER A SPRING HEARTFELT AND LONG,
WRITTEN DURING THE SECLUSION FAST

Thirty days of fasting and sitting *ch'an*
while neighbors enjoy pipe and song:

Moon radiant through wineless nights,
eyes all darkness gazing into blossoms,

I trust myself to this insight emptiness,
fathom how deeply thoughts are dust.

But I still think of idle talk and laughter,
and can't forget loved ones of long ago,

how I've been silent host at Lung-men
and often a guest in the Gardens of T'u,

that play of streamwater singing all day,
candles lit through snowbound nights.

Everything scatters away. Everything.
I keep wondering at this body still here

amid so much abandoned wind and light
this spring of my seventy-fourth year.

WONDERING ABOUT MIND: PRESENTED TO FRIENDS WHO'VE GROWN OLD

I wonder in the mornings what this mind could be thinking
and wonder in the evenings what this mind could be doing.

No longer running an office, hands tucked lazily into sleeves,
no longer looking after people, face free of worry and grief:

I stay home now, a recluse at ease. Here, it's mostly just sleep.
And though I've lost interest in that drinking of long ago,

I'll talk idly on and on with visiting friends who've grown old,
tenderly ladling out wine and offering them each a quiet cup.

Mind no longer searches for things scattered past and away,
and now that this body is rarely anything but tranquil ease,

it's done worrying over the body too. Now, whenever I wonder
what remains of mind, I find something beyond all knowing.

OFF-HAND POEM WRITTEN DURING THE SECLUSION FAST

Replenishing the censor, a servant
adds one stick of fragrant incense,

and I can still sit up, keep the bed
half clean with my deer-tail whisk.

Moving into my library for the sun,
I raise blinds, gaze into azure skies

and savor fruit tarts, fresh and sweet,
keeping warm in gentle old robes.

In easy contentment a tranquil life,
in idleness aplenty a joyful nature:

I don't cling to *yes this* and *no that*
or resist the play of motion and rest,

so what can tangle me in this world?
Heart empty, forgetfulness replete,

I'm old and sick and free of worry:
Mind is the master of its own cures.

NOTES

EARLY POEMS: 794-815 (C.E.)

3   **Meng Hao-jan:** The first of the great T'ang Dynasty poets, Meng Hao-jan (689-740) is known as a recluse poet who lived apart on Deer-Gate Mountain.

4   **Empty Gate:** empty mind, the gate through which englightenment is attained. Also, a name for Buddhism.

5   **mystery of solitude:** A term rich with the secular spirituality of Taoism and Ch'an, *yu* is more often rendered as "isolate mystery" in this book, and it might also be translated: "secret beauty" or "hidden mystery."

6   **month:** In the Chinese lunar calendar, the first day of the year corresponds to the beginning of spring. It falls on a different day every year, somewhere between late January and late February. Then through the year, each three month period corresponds to a season.
     ch'i: The universal breath, vital energy, or life-giving principle.

8   *Ch'ang-an* (Italicized city names indicate where poems that follow were written.)
     heaven: *Heaven's* most primitive meaning is simply "sky." By extension, it came to mean "transcendence," and then "fate" or "destiny." But Chuang Tzu added "natural process" to the weave of meaning, or more descriptively: the spontaneous unfolding of things which is natural process. This was

a response to his understanding that earth's natural process is itself both our fate in life and our transcendence, for self is but a fleeting form taken on by earth's process of change– born out of it, and returned to it in death.

9   **mind:** In ancient China, there was no fundamental distinction between heart and mind (see Introduction p. xiv). In Po Chü-i this range of meaning often blends into the technical use of *mind* in Ch'an Buddhism, where it means consciousness emptied of all content, or perhaps consciousness as empty awareness. But it also refers to an absolute realm of which consciousness partakes. For Po Chü-i, who made little fundamental distinction between Taoism and Ch'an, this realm was also the void out of which all things are engendered.

10   **Flowering-Brightness Monastery:** A monastery in Ch'ang-an named after a princess whose home it had been two centuries earlier. She was the daughter of Emperor T'ai-tsung (note to p. 21), the sage emperor who founded the T'ang Dynasty and whose benevolent rule contrasted so sharply with that of Po Chü-i's own age.
Phoenix: The phoenix appears only in times of peace and sagacious rule.

12   **cicadas:** The cicada recurs often in Po Chü-i's poems. In China, the cicada begins singing as summer turns to autumn, so its lovely voice evokes the melancholy beauty of autumn.

14   *Chou-chih*

16   *Ch'ang-an*
ch'in: ancient stringed instrument which Chinese poets used to accompany the chanting of their poems. It is ancestor to the more familiar Japanese *koto*.

17   **crane:** From its appearance in flight, the crane came to represent a kind of effortless freedom beyond the human realm, a masterful soaring in the timeless realm of natural process. Or more reductively: it can simply be a symbol for longevity and immortality.

feast on ferns: Esteemed recluses of the twelfth century B.C.E., Po Yi and Shu Ch'i refused even to eat the grain of a corrupt government. They retired to the mountains where they lived on ferns until they finally died of cold and hunger.

18 **New *Yüeh-fu*:** See Introduction p. xviii-xix.

21 **Emperor T'ai-tsung:** the man who founded the T'ang Dynasty and reigned as a sage emperor from 627 to 650. His best known saying is: "By using a mirror of brass you may see to adjust your cap. But by using the mirror of antiquity, you may learn to foresee the rise and fall of empires."

22 The proliferation of monasteries had become a serious social problem. They supported a huge parasitic population of monks who had no qualification or commitment to Buddhist practice. They had also accumulated vast amounts of wealth and land. In addition to leaving peasants with less and less, this represented a serious drain on the treasury because monasteries were not taxed. See Introduction p. xxi.

26 **South Mountain:** Calling up such passages as "like the timelessness of South Mountain" in *The Book of Songs* (*Shih Ching*, 166/6), South Mountain came to have a kind of mythic stature as the embodiment of the elemental and timeless nature of the earth.

28 **sitting:** sitting Ch'an meditation. See note to p. 100.

34 *Hsia-kuei*

40 **Foxglove:** herb capable of making animals glow dramatically with health. It was used, for instance, to make old horses appear healthy when being sold.

45 *Ch'ang-an*
     on a whim: The recluse Wang Hui-chih (d. 388) set out "on a whim" to visit a friend. When he arrived at the friend's house, however, the mood had vanished, so he simply returned home without seeing his friend.

53   *Hsün-yang*

62   There is also a celebrated prose version of this poem: "Record of a Thatched Hut." This prose version is available in Burton Watson's *Four Huts* and Richard Strassberg's *Inscribed Landscapes*.

64   **Ch'i-sited:** It was thought that the different features of a landscape determine the movement of *ch'i*, the universal breath. The best site for a house would be determined by a diviner who analyzed how the local movements of *ch'i* harmonized with the particular characteristics of those who will live in the house.

82   *Chung-chou*

87   **East Slope:** When Su Tung-p'o, the great Sung Dynasty poet, was exiled and living at East Slope, it is said he was thinking of this and several other Po Chü-i poems from this period when he took East Slope *(Tung- p'o)* as his literary name.

80   ***samādhi:*** a meditative state in which mental activity is stilled, leaving consciousness emptied of both experiencing subject and experienced object.

MIDDLE POEMS: 820-829

93   *Ch'ang-an*

98   **Boundless and free:** from the title of the first chapter in *Chuang Tzu*.
     Kalpa: In Ch'an Buddhism, the term for an endlessly long period of time. Originally, in Vedic scripture, a kalpa was a world-cycle lasting 4,320,000 years.

100   *Hang-chou*

ch'an: the sitting meditation more commonly known in the West by its Japanese name *zazen*. Or to make the terminology more precise: *ch'an* corresponds to *zen*, and *tso-ch'an* (sitting *ch'an*) corresponds to *za-zen* (sitting *zen*). The Ch'an school takes this as its name because it focuses on this meditation practice. See also the Introduction, especially pp. xiii-xiv.

102 **DarkEnigma:** DarkEnigma Learning, a philosophical school which arose in the third and fourth centuries C.E., gave Chinese thought a decidedly ontological turn and became central to the synthesis of Taoism and Buddhism into Ch'an Buddhism. DarkEnigma might be described as the generative ontological tissue from which the ten thousand things spring. According to Kuo Hsiang, one of the leading DarkEnigma philosophers: dwelling there,

> *no-mind inhabits the mystery of things. . . . This is the importance of being at the hinge of Tao: There you can know DarkEnigma's extent. There your movements range free.*

108 ***sorrow forgotten:*** Day lilies were also called the *sorrow-forgotten* flower.

110 *Lo-yang*

113 *Su-chou*

Master Jung Ch'i: Taoist hermit (Jung Ch'i-ch'i) of the fifth century B.C.E. Legend records an encounter with Confucius in which Confucius is deeply impressed when Jung Ch'i plays his *ch'in*, for he heard in the music such sage contentment with the wonder of life.

Chung Tzu-ch'i: Po Ya was a legendary *ch'in* player in ancient times, and Chung Tzu-ch'i was such a connoisseur and kindred spirit that he understood Po Ya at the most profound level when he played. When Po Ya played *mountains*, Chung saw T'ai Mountain rise before him. When Po Ya played *water*, Chung saw rivers flowing. Upon Chung's death, Po Ya broke his strings and smashed his *ch'in*, and never played again.

121 *Ch'ang-an*

123 **darnel:** A weed that grows in grain fields.

124 **red dust:** insubstantial worldly affairs.

125 **Seclusion Fast:** There were several months in the year when officials might live in retirement and generally focus attention on their spiritual lives, eating a simple meatless diet and spending much of their time sitting in Ch'an meditation.
three spirits: we are supposedly inhabited by three spirits which animate body, emotion, and reason.

126 *Flower-Garland:* name (Hua-yen) of a major sutra and school of Buddhism.
prajñā-**wisdom:** or *prajñā*, an immediately experienced intuitive wisdom that cannot be conveyed in intellectual terms. This insight into emptiness as the true nature of reality may be equated with the attainment of enlightenment.

LATE POEMS: 829-846

131 *Lo-yang*

132 **Lü-Tao District:** the district of Lo-yang where Po Chü-i's house was located.
ch'in **thoroughly strung:** There is a legend, meant to illustrate the state of T'ao Ch'ien's enlightenment, in which he plays his *ch'in* without any strings. T'ao Ch'ien (365-427 C.E.) was one of the most important Chinese poets, and a poet who influenced Po Chü-i greatly.

136 In ancient China, New Year's Day was not only the earth's "birth day," as it was the first day of spring, but the people all considered it their birthday as well. Hence, Po Chü-i has just turned sixty.

137 **Lung-men:** A lovely river valley with hills and cliffs, six miles south of Lo-yang. There are numerous monasteries there, including several where Po Chü-i often practiced in his years at Lo-yang, and some colossal sculptures carved from the cliffs (including a thirty-five-foot Buddha) which are among the glories of Chinese Buddhist sculpture.

139 **three noble-minded joys:** from *Mencius* XIII.20:

> *Mencius said: "The noble-minded have three great joys, and ruling all beneath Heaven is not one of them. To have parents alive and brothers well– that is the first joy. To face Heaven above and people below without any shame– that is the second joy. To attract the finest students in all beneath Heaven, and to teach and nurture them– that is the third joy. The noble-minded have three great joys, and ruling all beneath Heaven is not one of them."*

141 **Master Jung Ch'i:** see note to p. 113.

Chieh Yü: The legendary madman of Ch'u who ridicules Confucius, Chieh Yü (Convergence CrazyCart) was the archetypal eccentric whose wild antics revealed not madness but deep wisdom. See *The Analects* XVIII.5 and *Chuang Tzu* chapters 1, 4, 7 (Hinton translation, pp. 5, 62, 105).

148 **tea-cake rolled into powder:** In T'ang times, tea was processed into cakes or bricks, then crushed into a powder with a roller when it was used.

149 **ShimmerWords:** ShimmerWords (LiteraryGlory is another possible translation) is a cluster of stars in Ursa Major, a kind of celestial incarnation of the literary arts.

150 **star falling:** meteorites were well-known in T'ang China.

origins: Part of the *ch'in*'s profound appeal was that, when played by a master, its music seemed to spring from the very source of it all. Cf. p. 35.

152 **cloud-mother:** mica, for which "cloud-petal" is another appellation.

154 **Hui Yüan:** A major figure in the history of Chinese Buddhism, Hui Yüan (334-416 C.E.) emphasized *dhyāna* (sitting meditation), teaching a form of Buddhism which contained the first glimmers of Ch'an.

155 **Duke Liu:** After being instrumental in the founding of the Han Dynasty, Duke Liu (Chang Liang: c. 200 B.C.E.) became an assiduous recluse.

Master Red Pine: After magically summoning heavy rains and saving the empire from drought, the legendary Red Pine (c. twenty-seventh century B.C.E.) was transformed into an immortal and lived as a timeless recluse in the mythical K'un-lun Mountains.

159 **Chang Han:** third-century poet known for saying that he would prefer a single cup of wine in this life to any amount of fame after he died.
Chi K'ang: third-century literati recluse devoted to Taoist pursuits.
wander boundless and free: see note to p. 98.

162 **Sung Mountain:** The highest of China's five sacred peaks, Sung Mountain's complex of thirty-six peaks lies just southeast of Lo-yang.

170 Po Chü-i's note: "I brought cranes and water lilies with me from Su-chou."

171 **Wind Sickness:** Po had just suffered a serious stroke. His mind was unaffected but his left leg was crippled.

177 **Home:** "At home," in Buddhist phraseology means to be a lay practictioner, and "leaving home" means to be a monk.

178 **Willow Branch:** one of several courtesans who Po Chü-i "set free" when he grew old.

179 **Dancing waists and singing sleeves:** Po Chü-i's courtesans.
Stringless _ch'in_: see note to p. 132.

FINDING LIST

Page	1. *Po Chü-i chi chien chiao*	2. *Po Chü-i chi*	3. *Po Hsiang-shan shih-chi*
17	57	20	1.12a
18	165	61	3.4a
21	204	73	4.1a
22	208	74	4.1b
23	221	78	4.3b
25	223	78	4.4a
26	227	79	4.4b
27	256	88	4.9a
28	480	173	9.4a
29	805	274	14.2b
30	92	33	2.4a
31	96	34	2.4b
32	477	172	9.3b
33	824	280	14.6a
34	846	286	14.9a
35	302	103	5.7b
36	320	113	6.3a
37	328	116	6.4b
38	59	21	1.12b
39	521	188	10.3b
40	54	19	1.12a
41	857	290	14.11a
42	848	287	14.9b
43	855	289	14.12a
44	336	120	6.7a
45	355	126	6.11a
46	919	309	15.9a
47	926	311	15.10b
51	951	318	15.14b
52	947	316	15.13b
53	647	232	12.5a
55	995	331	16.5b
56	1009	336	16.8a

Page	1. *Po Chü-i chi chien chiao*	2. *Po Chü-i chi*	3. *Po Hsiang-shan shih-chi*
57	1010	336	16.8b
58	1014	338	16.9a
59	554	200	10.10a
60	371	132	7.3b
61	1026	341	16.11b
62	384	137	7.6a
64	1028	342	16.11b
65	1029	342	16.12a
66	1052	349	16.16a
67	401	143	7.10a
68	1045	346	16.15a
69	1092	361	17.7a
70	562	203	10.11b
71	1090	360	17.6b
72	1031	343	16.12b
73	1075	356	17.4a
74	508	182	9.9a
75	76	27	1.16a
77	1083	358	17.5b
78	1116	368	17.11a
79	568	205	10.12b
80	567	205	10.12b
81	407	145	7.11b
82	591	212	11.3a
83	1163	382	18.3a
84	614	220	11.8a
85	1192	391	18.8a
86	1198	393	18.9a
87	599	215	11.5a
89	1196	392	18.9a
93	644	231	12.4a
94	1261	412	19.6b
95	624	225	11.10b

Page	1. *Po Chü-i chi chien chiao*	2. *Po Chü-i chi*	3. *Po Hsiang-shan shih-chi*
97	1218	400	12.16b
98	625	225	11.10b
99	1315	428	20.1a
100	1319	430	20.2a
101	424	152	8.3a
102	1346	438	20.6b
103	699	244	12.11b
104	1371	445	25.4a
105	1389	451	25.7b
106	1392	452	25.8a
107	1392	452	25.8a
108	447	161	21.4b
109	448	161	21.5a
110	458	164	21.6b
111	455	163	21.6a
112	1599	523	26.9a
113	1634	535	27.4b
114	1653	540	27.8b
115	1656	541	27.8b
116	1423	461	21.12b
118	1670	546	27.11a
119	1682	549	27.13b
120	1441	469	21.16b
121	1710	558	28.2b
122	1712	559	28.3a
123	1719	561	28.4a
124	1763	573	28.11a
125	1792	582	29.2a
126	1843	596	19.10a
127	1841	598	19.10a
131	1492	489	22.8a
132	1744	568	28.8a
133	1769	575	8.12a

Page	1. *Po Chü-i chi chien chiao*	2. *Po Chü-i chi*	3. *Po Hsiang-shan shih-chi*
134	1890	613	29.15a
135	1884	611	29.14a
136	1971	643	30.10a
137	1904	620	31.1b
138	1954	637	30.6b
139	1965	641	30.9a
140	1971	644	30.10a
141	1967	642	30.9b
142	1976	646	30.11a
143	1776	577	8.13b
144	1849	600	31.6b
145	1518	499	22.13b
146	1863	604	39.2a
147	2267	746	34.6b
148	1859	603	31.9b
149	2132	702	32.6a
150	2110	695	32.2b
151	2136	704	32.7a
152	2161	712	32.11b
153	2150	708	32.9a
154	2019	662	23.5b
155	2062	678	24.3b
156	2173	716	33.1a
157	2222	731	33.10b
158	2241	737	34.1b
159	2039	668	23.9b
160	2169	715	32.13a
162	2248	740	34.3a
163	2043	670	23.10b
165	2271	748	34.7b
166	2047	672	23.11a
167	2236	735	33.12b
168	2003	656	23.2a

Page	1. *Po Chü-i chi chien chiao*	2. *Po Chü-i chi*	3. *Po Hsiang-shan shih-chi*
169	2316	762	34.16a
170	2368	779	35.10b
171	2387	787	36.1a
172	2388	788	36.1b
173	2389	788	36.1b
174	2390	789	36.2a
175	2409	796	36.5b
176	2435	804	36.10b
177	2426	802	36.8b
178	2572	853	37.14b
179	2427	802	36.9a
180	2482	821	24.15a
181	2509	830	37.3a
182	2485	822	24.15b
183	2487	823	24.16a
184	2561	850	37.13b
185	2578	855	37.16a
186	2580	856	37.16b

FURTHER READING

Ch'en, Kenneth. *The Chinese Transformation of Buddhism*. Princeton: Princeton University Press, 1973.

Levy, Howard. *Translations from Po Chü-i's Collected Works*. 4 vols. Taipei: Chinese Materials Center, 1970-78.

Neinhauser, William. *The Indiana Companion to Traditional Chinese Literature*. Bloomington: Indiana University Press, 1986.

Strassberg, Richard. *Inscribed Landscapes: Travel Writing from Imperial China*. Berkeley: University of California Press, 1994.

Waley, Arthur. *Chinese Poems*. London: George Allen & Unwin, 1946.

——. *The Life and Times of Po Chü-i*. London: George Allen & Unwin, 1949.

Watson, Burton. "Buddhism in the Poetry of Po Chü-i," *The Eastern Buddhist*, 21.1 (1988).

——. *Chinese Lyricism*. New York: Columbia University Press, 1971.

——. *Four Huts*. Boston: Shambhala Publications, 1994.